The Corporate Culture
Survival Guide

The Corporate Culture Survival Guide

New and Revised Edition

Edgar H. Schein

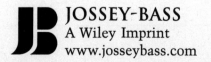
JOSSEY-BASS
A Wiley Imprint
www.josseybass.com

Published by Jossey-Bass
A Wiley Imprint
989 Market Street, San Francisco, CA 94103–1741   www.josseybass.com

Jossey-Bass books and products are available through most bookstores. To contact Jossey-Bass
directly call our Customer Care Department within the U.S. at 800–956–7739, outside the U.S.
at 317–572–3986, or fax 317–572–4002.

Jossey-Bass also publishes its books in a variety of electronic formats. Some content that appears
in print may not be available in electronic books.

Library of Congress Cataloging-in-Publication Data
Schein, Edgar H.
    The corporate culture survival guide / Edgar H. Schein.—New and rev. ed.
        p.   cm.
    Includes bibliographical references and index.
    ISBN 978-0-470-29371-3 (cloth)
        1. Corporate culture.   2. Culture.   3. Organizational behavior.   I. Title.
    HD58.7.S3217   2009
    658.4'06—dc22
                                                            2009011482

Printed in the United States of America
NEW AND REVISED EDITION
HB Printing   10 9

Warren Bennis

A WARREN BENNIS BOOK
This collection of books is devoted exclusively to new
and exemplary contributions to management thought
and practice. The books in this series are addressed to
thoughtful leaders, executives, and managers of all
organizations who are struggling with and committed
to responsible change. My hope and goal is to spark
new intellectual capital by sharing ideas positioned at
an angle to conventional thought—in short, to publish
books that disturb the present in the service of a
better future.

Books in the Warren Bennis Signature Series

Branden	*Self-Esteem at Work*
Mitroff, Denton	*A Spiritual Audit of Corporate America*
Schein	*The Corporate Culture Survival Guide*
Sample	*The Contrarians Guide to Leadership*
Lawrence, Nohria	*Driven*
Cloke, Goldsmith	*The End of Management and the Rise of Organizational Democracy*
Glen	*Leading Geeks*
Cloke, Goldsmith	*The Art of Waking People Up*
George	*Authentic Leadership*
Kohlrieser	*Hostage at the Table*
Rhode	*Moral Leadership*
George	*True North*
Townsend	*Up the Organization*
Kellerman, Rhode	*Women and Leadership*
Riggio	*The Art of Followership*
Gergen, Vanourek	*Life Entrepreneurs*
Frohman, Howard	*Leadership the Hard Way*
George, McLean, Craig	*Finding Your True North: A Personal Guide*
Kleiner	*The Age of Heretics*
Cleveland	*Nobody in Charge*
Higgins	*Career imprints*
Burke, Lake, Paine	*Organization Change*
Zaffran, Logan	*The Three Laws of Performance*

Contents

Preface to the New and Revised Edition

The field of organizational culture has evolved along several dimensions in the ten years since the first edition of this book. This new and revised edition attempts to capture this evolution while retaining the fundamental model of culture that continues to prove to be a useful tool. My basic model of organizational culture has not changed, but the application of the model has certainly changed both research and practice around culture formation, evolution, and managed change. I am still addressing the practicing leader and manager who wants to understand and work with culture. To that end the basic structure of the book will look similar to the first edition.

Culture as a concept in organizational life has come to be accepted, but there is still a strong divide between (1) those who want very abstract universal dimensions of culture that can be measured with surveys and questionnaires and (2) those who want to study the nuances, details, and dynamics of particular cultures by observation, interview, and intervention. The first approach looks for general traits; the second approach looks for general cultural processes.

Both groups are interested in how cultural forces impact organizational performance, but whereas the first group is looking for cultural traits that will correlate with performance across all kinds of companies and industries, the second group is looking for direct linkages between particular cultural events and performance outcomes. The first approach lends itself to a quantitative cross-sectional analysis, the second requires a more clinical longitudinal analysis. The first approach of necessity develops variables that are quite abstract and removed from here-and-now organizational events that the manager or consultant encounters in a particular company. The second approach looks for proximate variables that enable the manager or consultant to deal with the immediate situation. The first approach tries to develop broad theoretical principles that apply to large numbers of organizations. The second approach looks for middle-level theories that illuminate local situations.

I have chosen to highlight this difference at the outset in order to make it very clear to the reader what my own position is on this dimension. While I gain some insight from the work of colleagues who work on the first approach, I have found that my own insights are far greater if I am clinically involved as an active change agent. I have come to believe that at this stage of the development of our field we still need the detailed clinical studies of cultural events because we do not yet know what the crucial dimensions and variables will ultimately turn out to be.

There is also a more pressing argument for the second approach. One cannot really build, evolve, or change culture without getting into the messy details of particular cultures. The broad dimensions are valid, but they are so distant from the day-to-day phenomena that leaders and managers are wrestling with that they do not inform you on what should be done.

So this book, especially this new and revised edition, is written to the leader and manager who needs to get something done and, therefore, needs to understand the nitty gritty of culture dynamics. As it turns out, this nitty gritty has become much more complex because of the evolution of technological complexity, leading to more occupational subcultures, and the growth of globalism, leading to more groups and organizations that mix both occupational and national cultures. A merger of two companies in one country is a far different set of issues than a joint venture of two different companies from two different countries trying to put together a project in yet another country.

Leaders and managers of organizations (and societies) are creators, products, and victims of culture. And it is one of the unique functions of leadership not only to create cultures in new groups but also to manage cultural issues in mature organizations. For all of this, they need concepts and a toolkit. This book is written from that point of view. It is intended to explain what culture is, when and how one assesses it, and when and how one changes it.

The basic structure is similar to the previous edition. In Part One we examine basic definitions, why culture is important in the first place, and what range of dimensions can be explored in probing the content of culture. Part Two begins with an important chapter on general change theory and how it applies to culture. In the next three chapters I explain how to work with culture at different stages of organizational evolution. Finally, we end with the very new issue of multicultural groups that more or less start from scratch to blend together to the extent possible the different assumptions that are brought to a new project by members from different cultures. This is as yet uncharted territory but some principles of how to blend cultures are beginning to emerge.

Acknowledgements

My main debt is once again to my clients, who not only provided endlessly interesting and challenging culture puzzles but whose efforts to evolve and change culture revealed many of the crucial dynamics that have informed the content of this book. Whenever possible I have named these clients, but in some projects confidentially was requested so I gave them pseudonyms.

I am very appreciative of the thoughtful and detailed reviews of my first edition that were provided by the Jossey-Bass editorial staff and want to express a special thank you to Joan Gallos, who was helpful as a reviewer and, more importantly, as a guide through the complexity of the reviews themselves.

Ed Schein
Cambridge, MA
January 2009

The Author

Ed Schein is the Sloan Fellows Professor of Management Emeritus at the MIT Sloan School of Management. He received his Ph.D. in social psychology from Harvard in 1952, worked at the Walter Reed Institute of Research for four years, and then joined MIT, where he taught until 2005. He has published extensively in organizational psychology (*Organizational Psychology*, 3rd ed., 1980), process consultation (*Process Consultation Revisited*, 1999), career dynamics (*Career Anchors*, 3rd ed., 2006), organizational culture texts (*Organizational Culture and Leadership*, 3rd ed., 2004), analyses of Singapore's economic miracle (*Strategic Pragmatism*, 1996), and Digital Equipment Corp.'s rise and fall (*DEC Is Dead; Long Live DEC*, 2003). He continues to consult and recently published a book on the general theory and practice of giving and receiving help (*Helping*, 2009).

Part One

THE STRUCTURE AND CONTENT OF CULTURE

In order to manage culture, you must understand what culture is, what content culture covers, and how to assess it. It is dangerous to oversimplify this concept because of the illusion that one is managing culture when one is, in fact, managing only a manifestation of culture and, therefore, not achieving one's change goals.

1

WHY BOTHER?

Why is it important to understand culture? In this chapter I will provide an overview of the many ways in which culture matters. First, culture and leadership are two sides of the same coin and one cannot understand one without the other. Next, we have to understand that organizations are cultural units that have within them powerful subcultures based on occupations and common histories. We have to recognize that organizations exist within broader cultural units that matter in today's global world because mergers, acquisitions, joint ventures and special projects are often multicultural entities who must have the ability to work across cultures. Finally, we have to understand that the culture issues are different in young, mid-life, and older organizations.

Leadership and Culture Are Intertwined

Not only does culture reside within us as individuals, but it is also the hidden force that drives most of our behavior both inside and outside organizations. We are members of a country, an occupation, an organization, a community, a family, and a social group. Each of these cultures is part of us and impacts us. In every new social situation, whether we are aware of it or not, we function as "leaders" in that we not only reinforce and act as a part of the present culture, but often begin to create new cultural elements. This interplay of culture creation, reenactment, and reinforcement creates an interdependency between culture and leadership.

Much of the confusion about what culture and leadership mean derives from a failure to consider this interaction between them and our failure to define what stage of an organization's life we are talking about. If the leader is an entrepreneur who is founding an organization, he or she will have the opportunity to begin the culture creation process by imposing beliefs, values, and assumptions onto new employees. If the new organization succeeds, then its cultural elements become shared and constitute the emerging culture of that organization. What is considered "leadership" then reflects what the founder imposed and will become the definition of what is considered appropriate leadership in that organization. A successful organization founded by a compulsive autocrat will consider that style of leadership as the "correct" way to run a company, just as another successful organization founded by a participative democrat will consider that style to be "correct." One reason why it is so hard to define leadership is that there are so many "correct" versions, each reflecting one of the many kinds of successful organizations that exist in the world, each with its own culture.

When new leaders take over existing organizations, they find that the existing culture defines what kind of leadership style is expected and accepted, based on past history and the beliefs, values, and assumptions of earlier leaders. This is true whether we are talking about a new political appointee taking over a government department, a new CEO taking over a business, or a new minister taking over a congregation. If the new leader has been promoted from within, he or she will have some sense of the cultural issues that need to be dealt with. However, if the new leader comes from outside the organization, he or she will have to choose among several options:

1. *Destroy the existing culture* by getting rid of the key culture carriers, usually the top two or three echelons of executives, and attempt to implement his or her own beliefs, values, and assumptions by arbitrarily imposing new behavioral rules on the remaining employees. The risk of using this alternative is that essential knowledge, skills, and "know-how" will be lost as well and the performance of the organization will decline.

2. *Fight the existing culture* by attempting to impose his or her own beliefs, values, and assumptions on the existing members of the organization. The risk of this alternative is that the organization will adapt only on the surface and "wait it out" until the leader is eventually replaced—the old culture usually will "win" in this scenario unless the new leader has extraordinary charisma.

3. *Give in to the existing culture* by abandoning his or her own beliefs, values, and assumptions. The risk of this alternative is that *all* of the elements of the old culture will be perpetuated when in fact some of these elements are obsolete and dysfunctional and should, therefore, be changed.

4. *Evolve the culture* by initially adapting enough to figure out how to get things done and then gradually imposing new rules and behaviors that rest on different beliefs, values, and assumptions. For many leaders and for many organizations, this is the desirable alternative in terms of improving effectiveness and it is the essence of what is meant by "culture change." For old and well-established organizations such as government departments or old industries, cultural evolution is the only possible alternative. The cultural dynamics underlying such evolution are the essence of what leaders as culture managers must learn, and these dynamics are the central theme of this book.

Subcultures

The leader's role in evolving the culture is complicated by the fact that, as organizations grow and mature, they not only develop their own overall cultures, but they also differentiate themselves into many subcultures based on occupations, product lines, functions, geographies, and echelons in the hierarchy. In some organizations the subcultures are as strong as or stronger than the overall organizational culture. Leaders thus must not only understand the cultural consequences of the many ways in which growing organizations differentiate themselves but, more importantly, must align the various subcultures that have been created toward a common corporate purpose.

Managing the alignment of many subcultures has become especially important in the 21st century because of:

- Mergers, acquisitions, and joint ventures in which the subcultures are actually entire organizational cultures that need to be blended or at least aligned

- Globalization, which produces many diverse multicultural organizational units based on nationality, language, and ethnicity

- Technological complexity, which produces many more "mature" occupational subcultures that have to be taken into account in designing the flow of work (Technological complexity implies that every functional unit such as finance, marketing, or R & D is now more specialized and is attracting members of occupations that are themselves more specialized.)

- Information technology, which has created many more structural options of when, where, and by whom work is to be done (Cultures tend to grow from the interaction of co-located employees, so the question arises of what kinds of subcultures can and will form in networks of employees who are electronically connected but may never have met each other.)

These cultural and subcultural issues influence all aspects of how an organization functions, so the task of leadership is to understand the dynamic forces that arise and to manage these forces to ensure that they are congruent with the organization's mission and goals. As subculture dynamics become more important, the role of leadership broadens. It is not enough for the CEO and the top executive group to be concerned about and manage the "corporate culture." Leaders at every level of the organization must recognize that they have a role in creating, managing, and evolving the subcultures in their parts of the organization. One obvious example is that union leadership must not only understand, manage, and evolve the union's culture, but must also ensure that the union, as a subculture, is aligned with the corporate culture of a unionized organization.

In summary, leadership cannot really be understood without consideration of cultural origins, evolution, and change. In the same way, organizational culture and subcultures cannot really be understood without considering how leaders at every level and in every function of an organization behave and influence how the total system functions. Organizational functioning is heavily dependent on how existing subcultures align with each other, which means that it is critical for leaders to understand and manage subculture dynamics.

Samples of How the Leadership/ Culture Interaction Matters

Many years ago, when Atari was preeminent in designing computerized games, they brought in a new CEO whose background was in marketing. His cultural background told him that the way to run a company was to get a good individual incentive and career system going. Imagine his chagrin when he discovered a loosely organized bunch of engineers and programmers whose work was so seemingly disorganized that you could not even tell whom to reward for what. The CEO was sure he knew how to clean up that kind of mess! He instituted clear personal accountabilities and an individualistic, competitive reward system symbolized by identifying the "engineer of the month"—only to discover that the organization became demoralized and some of the best engineers left the company.

This well-meaning CEO had not realized that in its evolution the company had learned that the essence of the creative process in designing good games was the unstructured collaborative climate that enabled designers to trigger each other's creativity. The successful game was a group product. The individual engineers shared an assumption that only through extensive informal interaction could an idea come to fruition. No one could recall who had actually contributed what. The new individualized reward system gave too much credit to the "engineer of the month" named by the CEO, and the competitive climate reduced the fun and creativity. This leader did not understand a crucial element of the culture he was entering, so he made some decisions that changed a key element of the culture in a dysfunctional way.

The story of Digital Equipment Corporation (DEC) will be told throughout this book, but for purposes of understanding how much culture matters it needs to be said at the outset that the very culture that made DEC a great company in a remarkably short period of time became dysfunctional as size, market conditions, and technology changed.[1] Ken Olsen as a leader created a remarkable culture in which all employees felt fully responsible and committed to the growth and success of the organization through innovating a whole new style of computing. One could interact with DEC computers online—the first time that this was possible.

Olsen's leadership created what became in the mid-1980s the second-largest computer company in the industry. It was a model of how to "empower" people and build a company through product innovation. But as technology and market forces changed in the 1980s toward the computer as a commodity, the DEC culture of innovation failed to adapt to changing technological and economic circumstances, leading to its sale to Compaq and eventual absorption into Hewlett-Packard (HP). Was this a failure of leadership, or was the culture now powerful enough to dictate what kind of leadership would be acceptable, even if it was economically dysfunctional?

The next story illustrates how long it takes to make substantial changes in part of the culture of a large organization—the conversion of Procter & Gamble's manufacturing system in the 1950s to become a low-cost producer. A far-sighted manager of manufacturing empowered a staff group to examine how one might reorganize plants to increase both productivity and worker satisfaction.[2] With the help of organization development (OD) consultants such as Douglas McGregor and Richard Beckhard, this staff group evolved a concept of a factory that depended much more on worker involvement and a reward system that emphasized multiple skills and job trading, rather than job specialization, hierarchical position, or number of people supervised. The essence of the idea was to have a plant view itself as a business with suppliers and customers, and to run that business responsibly. To achieve that would require not only changing some elements of the corporate culture but, more importantly, to change key elements of the union culture. Workers would become multi-skilled and supportive of each other throughout the operation, instead of having rigid rules about who does what.

The staff group also realized that there was no chance of selling such a concept either to the union or to more traditional management types. They had to start with a new plant, hire their own plant manager, and teach him the new concept of a plant as a self-managing business. A leader was found who embodied these new beliefs and the "Augusta" plant was born. It was highly successful, but to proliferate this success the staff group decided that potential managers of other new plants (and of the old, unionized plants) would have to learn the new system in an apprenticeship capacity to ensure that they really understood it. New kinds of leaders with different kinds of management attitudes had to be trained if the new management system was to be embedded in the new and old plants.

Over the next several years, a number of new plants started up, in each case with a manager who had apprenticed in the Augusta plant. The new operations worked well and built new cultures based on productivity and involvement, but the unionized plants remained problematic because of well-established cultures based on years of conflict-full labor/management interaction. Some of the older-and-wiser ex-Augusta managers were then placed into those plants to begin the process of "changing the culture," although that was not the terminology used at the time. Each plant also had an "organization development" (OD) manager who reported directly to the plant manager. These OD managers had been recruited from the employee ranks before being trained in organization development on the theory that they would understand the union culture better and, therefore, have more credibility as change agents.

My work with one of these managers highlighted the problem. Until the union began to trust management, there was no chance of even discussing the new kinds of production systems that would allow for job trading and multi-skilling—notions that violated some of the most sacred cows of trade unionism. In one plant, it took about five years for the union to decide that the manager could be trusted and to open discussion of a new kind of contract. After several more years, the union accepted the new system and saw that it was of benefit to all. In the mid-1990s, I attended a celebration marking the conversion of the last of P&G's unionized plants to the new system. The event occurred fifteen years after the launch of the Augusta plant, but a real culture change had been achieved in the manufacturing division through a carefully designed and managed process of culture evolution.

"Acme Insurance" (a pseudonym) illustrates the consequences of changing technology without analyzing the constraints of culture and the interaction of subcultures. Acme decided to increase its competitiveness by rapidly evolving to the paperless office with all major transactions to be done by computer in the very near future.[3] To accomplish this change, they hired a talented manager of information technology (IT) who had a proven track record in implementing new systems. She was given a tough target of converting the clerical staff to the new paperless system within one year. Training modules were created to teach employees how to use the new system effectively. But the IT manager was not aware that the company was, at the same time, launching intensive productivity efforts that signaled to the employees that they had to get their normal work done in addition to whatever training they could squeeze in. The subculture of production was not aligned with the subculture of IT.

The result was that the training was done in off hours and half-heartedly and, worse, the IT manager was not told this because the employees feared senior management reprisal. At the end of the year, the IT manager announced that the paperless transaction system had been successfully installed, but she did not know that the employees were so poorly trained that it was taking them much longer to use the computers than it had taken to use paper. Productivity actually dropped. Failure to recognize some of the deep realities of their own corporate culture and its subcultures caused this organization to waste tremendous amounts of money and effort for very little gain.

I observed a similar scenario in the back room of a large bank that installed computerized recordkeeping to reduce paper flow. Employees had data on their computer screens, but when a customer called with an inquiry, there was never enough of the case history on a single screen for the employee to rely on. So the employees kept extensive backup folders, which they pulled out and spread out on their desks as needed. Whenever the IT-oriented manager came around, the folders disappeared and the employees pretended to be using only the computers. This was not a technology failure. It was a managerial failure to understand the subculture operating in the clerical group.

Subculture issues in another kind of organizational context are illustrated when large "accidents" occur. For example, the shooting down of the UN helicopters in Iraq's no-fly zone in 1994 with the loss of twenty-six UN peacekeepers can best be explained by multiple communication failures between the Army helicopters, the Air Force fighters who guarded the no-fly zone, and the high flying Air Force AWACS, who were supposed to monitor all traffic in the area.[4] These communication failures resulted primarily because the cultures of these organizations had different priorities, which led to gradual drifting apart of the communication systems they used. A similar argument has been made in explaining the failure of NASA to cancel the ill-fated Challenger launch, even though several members of the engineering subculture argued strongly that the O-rings would fail in cold weather.[5]

Subculture issues become important in mergers, acquisitions, and joint ventures. When organizations that have developed their own cultures acquire each other, attempt to merge, or engage in various kinds of partnerships and joint ventures, the culture issue is more blatant and visible. However, surprisingly little attention is paid to culture before the new organization is created, and it is often a surprise to the parent company that it now has to deal with powerful subcultures that may not blend together very well. As the new organization begins to function, people hear the rhetoric that "we will take the best from both cultures," but that is usually not possible because each subculture will continue to support its own way of doing things.

I recently spoke to a senior executive from Novartis, which is the merger of Sandoz and Ciba-Geigy, two Swiss chemical/ pharmaceutical companies. I had worked with Ciba-Geigy in the 1970s and was surprised to learn of this merger because at that time the companies were actively competing with each other. When I asked the Novartis executive how the merger was working, he pointed out that it was going fine between the parent companies, but that there were still Ciba people and Geigy people who did not get along. This may well reflect the fact that when Ciba and Geigy merged in 1971 they had to blend together several different technologies reflecting different occupational subcultures, whereas the Novartis merger reflected more the blending of what had become two pharmaceutical companies with similar technologies.

In these cases it is most important to recognize that different occupations reflect different cultures based on the education and training of the people in those occupations. These differences have always been acknowledged in the way that companies tend to protect and isolate their research and development departments, often physically moving them to remote locations. What is just recently being recognized is that finance, marketing, engineering, manufacturing, and the other major business functions develop different subcultures because the members of these functions have different occupational backgrounds. The best way to understand subcultures is, therefore, to examine the backgrounds of the people who make up the groups that are at issue.

Merger Options

In cases in which cultures have to be combined, four possible patterns may evolve: *separation, domination, blending,* or *conflict.*[6]

Separation. The first possible option is that the cultures remain separate, as happens when conglomerates allow subsidiary companies to retain their separate identities. I was asked some years ago by the Swedish government to run a workshop for the senior executives of the government-owned Swedish industries to decide whether they should launch an effort to create a "common culture" across their various industries. After lengthy discussion of the disparate elements of ship building, mining, bottled water, and so on, it was clear that a common culture was not only a bad idea but probably impossible to implement. The attendees did agree that the senior executives in each industry should be viewed as "corporate property" and be made available in whatever industry needed them. But even there, they decided it would be dangerous to remove these executives from the companies in which they had achieved success.

Separation can work if the cultures are "aligned" in the sense of not working at cross-purposes with each other. This is easy if the owners manage through limited financial linkages. It becomes more difficult in partnerships or joint ventures in which the parents have different cultures.

Domination. The second possibility is that one culture dominates the other. In some cases this is explicit, as when one company openly acquires another. When Intel bought a semiconductor plant from DEC in the early 1990s, the new management announced that the plant would now operate by the Intel method—and that was that! When Hewlett-Packard bought Apollo, it coercively trained Apollo employees to adopt "the HP way." I learned from a group of engineers in Palo Alto that the HP way required people to be nice to each other and reach consensus in group meetings. If you resisted too vigorously, they said the boss would pull you aside later and tell you that you were "not a team player." Some months later, I was sitting next to a young woman who had gone to work for Apollo in Massachusetts; I asked her how she liked it. She said it was OK, but she worried that one could not really be outspoken or get one's point of view across. I asked her what would happen if she persisted in arguing for her view, and she said—literally—"The boss will pull you aside and tell you that you are not a team player!!!"

Does one see less domination in so-called mergers of equals? Or is every merger an acquisition—no matter what the rhetoric is about taking the best from each culture? In my own experience, one culture is always dominant, but this reality may not be visible for some time—precisely because of the rhetoric.

Blending. Can cultures blend or integrate? Blending, taking the best of each culture, is usually claimed to be the desirable outcome. What happens in practice is generally more complex and questionable. One level of blending is to create a new, superimposed set of values and sell them to the various cultural units. As we will see in later chapters, this only works under certain conditions. At another level, the new organization attempts to benchmark its various systems and procedures against each other and against externally perceived "best practices" to create and standardize new procedures across the resultant organization. One often hears that the new organization takes the accounting system from one parent, the human resource system from the other parent, and so on.

To balance power and maintain the image of merging, the board chairman often comes from one company and the president from the other, or a succession system is announced that draws senior people alternatively from each organization. These moves preserve the public image of a merger, but it cannot be inferred from the standardizing of systems that the cultures actually blend. In fact, the often-seen resistance to changes in the new organization is almost always based on the fact that cultural issues have not been considered at all in making decisions about procedures. In one merger, it was found that a company paid very high salaries but aggressively resisted stock options and other forms of golden handcuffs because of a deep belief that one should neither provide promises of lifetime employment nor expect loyalty from employees. The other company had grown up with the belief that people needed to be developed as long-range resources and therefore had adopted a low-salary, high-stock-option and high-bonus system. There was no way to blend these two philosophies. One had to win out over the other.

Blending is most likely to occur when the separate subcultures face a new common problem that can only be solved by collaboration. When members of the subcultures have to work together in forced interaction, they begin to pay attention to each other, develop understanding of their differences, and create new ways of working that take advantage of both cultures.

Though blending is often a desired outcome, especially in joint ventures or partnerships, in a study of fifty-fifty (ownership) joint ventures with parents from different countries, very little evidence of initial blending was found. Only when the joint venture faced a crisis that required real collaboration was there any evidence of blending.[7]

Conflict Resistance and "Counter-Culture." Not every subculture is aligned with the corporate mission and the corporate culture. This phenomenon becomes most noticeable in the destructive behavior of some unions whose goals are so out of line with what corporate headquarters would consider that they actually are willing to jeopardize their own jobs in trying to bring the company down. However, to varying degrees one sees subcultures that oppose at least some elements of the corporate culture in every organization. Sometimes these subcultures cause internally stimulated revolutions, as when a military group takes over a government by force.

Conflicts are often viewed as "power plays" or "politics," as when engineering and manufacturing fight or when marketing and finance get into conflict, but what is missed in that construction is the important fact that it is subcultures with different views that are in conflict with each other, not individual managers. Even if the senior managers agreed, there is no guarantee that the members of the subcultures would understand each other enough to be able to implement what was decided.

How Culture Matters at Different Stages of Growth

Culture matters in different ways according to the stages of organizational evolution. A young and growing company attempts to stabilize and proliferate the culture that it views as the basis of its success. The culture is the main source of the organization's identity and is therefore clung to with a vengeance, just as adolescents cling to their budding identities. Young organizations are also typically still under the control of their founders, which means the culture is more or less a reflection of the founder's beliefs and values. Even if success leads to broader acceptance of those beliefs and values across the whole population, one must recognize that a challenge to any cultural element is tantamount to questioning the founder or owners of the organization. Those cultural elements become sacred cows and are difficult to change. Culture "change" is therefore more a matter of evolving and reinforcing cultural elements, as will be explained later.

A mid-life organization can be defined as an organization that has had at least two generations of professional managers appointed by outside boards whose members are usually beholden to diverse stockholders. Most likely such an organization evolves into multiple units based on functions, products, markets, or geographies, and those units are likely to develop subcultures of their own. Thus the culture issue in the mid-life organization is threefold:

1. How to maintain those elements of the culture that continue to be adaptive and relate to the organization's success;

2. How to integrate, blend, or at least align the various subcultures; and

3. How to identify and change those cultural elements that may be increasingly dysfunctional as external environmental conditions change.

In such a mature organization, one will find a corporate culture that reflects all the parts of the organization and many subcultures that reflect functions, products, markets, and geographies. An overall assessment of the culture could become very cumbersome, therefore, because the culture will have so many elements and facets. However, as we will see, assessment of the culture's strengths and weaknesses becomes important when the organization is trying to change strategy or business processes. Culture assessment can then be geared to the business changes that are being proposed in order to discover how the present culture and subcultures will aid or hinder the proposed changes.

As companies age, elements of the corporate culture or the misalignment of subcultures can become serious survival problems for the organization, especially if the technology, market conditions, and financial situation have changed. Key elements of the corporate culture can become a serious constraint on learning and change. The organization clings to whatever made it a success. The very culture that created the success makes it difficult for members of the organization to perceive changes in the environment that require new responses. Culture becomes a constraint on strategy.

An aircraft company that nearly went bankrupt with one of its commercial models subsequently became highly successful in the defense industry and evolved a corporate culture that was well adapted to working with the government. New opportunities for commercial aircraft arose, but the board and senior management were now unable even to contemplate going back into the commercial business because of their strong memories of the debacle several decades earlier and their comfort with their present culture.

The culture issue in the older maladapted company is how to engage in massive transformations, often under great time pressure to avoid serious economic damage. The process of transformation is basically the same as in the healthy mid-life company, but the demands of time and the amount of change needed often precipitate drastic measures (usually labeled "turn-arounds"). Rapid unlearning and letting go of things that are valued is for many employees too difficult; either they leave the organization or they are let go because they "resist change" too strongly. If the attempt to manage the change fails, the organization may go bankrupt—and start all over again, building a new culture with new management, or be acquired and find a new culture imposed on it.

How cultural evolution and transformative change can be managed will be discussed later in this book.

Where Does Culture Reside?

Culture is a property of a group. Whenever a group has enough common experience, a culture begins to form. One finds cultures at the level of small teams, families, and work groups. Cultures also arise at the level of departments, functional groups, and other organizational units that have a common occupational core and common experience. Cultures are found at every hierarchical level. Culture exists at the level of the whole organization if there is sufficient shared history. It is even found at the level of a whole industry because of the shared occupational backgrounds of the people industry-wide. Finally, culture exists at the level of regions and nations because of common language, ethnic background, religion, and shared experience.

You as an individual, therefore, are a multicultural entity and are able to display different cultural behaviors depending on what the situation elicits. But if you spend the bulk of your life in a given occupation and organization, you not only take on many of the cultural themes that others in the occupation or organization share, but these become tacit assumptions and drop out of your awareness. It is this unconscious quality of culture that makes it so powerful. You are not aware of your cultural biases until someone challenges them or until you have offended someone with a different cultural background.

The Bottom Line

Culture matters because it is a powerful, tacit, and often unconscious set of forces that determine both our individual and collective behavior, ways of perceiving, thought patterns, and values. Organizational culture in particular matters because cultural elements determine strategy, goals, and modes of operating.

The values and thought patterns of leaders and senior managers are partially determined by their own cultural backgrounds and their shared experiences. If we want to make organizations more efficient and effective, then we must understand the role that culture plays in organizational life. If we want leadership to be more effective, we have to make leaders aware of their unique role as culture creators, evolvers, and managers.

Having thought broadly about culture, it is now time to think more precisely about how to define culture, how to assess it, and how to begin to evolve it.

Questions for the Reader

As you begin to think about culture, think about it first in your own personality:

- Review your family, ethnic, national, and educational background to identify the major influences on your current values and ways of doing things.

- Review your current formal and informal group affiliations to identify what current norms and values matter to you.

- Think about your place of work, its history, and traditions and see how that relates to your own values and ways of doing things.

2

WHAT IS CULTURE ANYWAY?

Three Levels of Culture

The biggest danger in trying to understand culture is to oversimplify it. It is tempting to say that culture is just "the way we do things around here," "the rites and rituals of our company," "the company climate," "the reward system," "our basic values," and so on. These are all manifestations of the culture, but none is the culture at the level where culture matters. A better way to think about culture is to realize that it exists at several "levels," and that we must understand and manage the deeper levels, as illustrated in Figure 2.1. The levels of culture go from the very visible to the very tacit and invisible.

Figure 2.1. The Three Levels of Culture

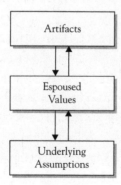

Artifacts — Visible organizational structures and processes (hard to decipher)

Espoused Values — Strategies, goals, philosophies (espoused justifications)

Underlying Assumptions — Unconscious, taken for granted beliefs, perceptions, thoughts, and feelings... (ultimate source of values and action)

Level One: Artifacts

The easiest level to observe when you go into an organization is that of artifacts—what you see, hear, and feel as you hang around. Think about restaurants, hotels, stores, banks, or automobile dealerships. Note your observations and emotional reactions to the architecture, the decor, and the climate, based on how people behave toward you and toward each other.

You can sense immediately that different organizations do things differently. For example, in Digital Equipment Corp. (DEC) people were constantly in meetings with each other, there were no walls or closed doors, they dressed informally, there was an intensity of feeling all around, and you got a sense of fast-paced action. In Ciba-Geigy, on the other hand, everything was very formal. People were behind closed doors, conversations were hushed, dress was formal, and you got a sense of careful deliberation and slow movement.

As a customer or new employee, you may like or dislike one or the other of these organizations; you may think to yourself that DEC and Ciba-Geigy have different cultures. But you have to be careful. All you know for sure is that they have different ways of presenting themselves and different norms of how to deal with each other. What you don't know is what this all means.

In other words, at the level of artifacts, culture is very clear and has immediate emotional impact. But you don't really know why the members of the organization are behaving as they do and why each organization is constructed as it is. Just by hanging around and observing, you cannot really decipher what is going on. Even when you see very similar things, you don't know whether they mean the same thing, as in the case of pyramids in Egypt and pyramids in Mayan Central America. You have to be able to talk to insiders and ask them questions about the things you observe and feel. That takes you to the next deeper level of culture.

Level Two: Espoused Values

Imagine yourself to be a new employee or manager, offered jobs at two companies that differ as much as DEC and Ciba-Geigy did. Should you go to work for the one whose entry lobby and security procedures make you feel most comfortable? Do you know enough about either culture from experiencing the artifacts and behavior patterns, or should you dig more deeply? To dig deeper means to start asking questions about the things the organization values. Why do they do what they do? Why did DEC create open office areas while Ciba-Geigy put everyone behind closed doors? These questions have to be asked, especially about those observed artifacts that puzzle you or that seem somehow inconsistent with what you would expect. For this purpose, you need to find insiders who can explain their organization to you. Anthropologists call them "informants" and depend heavily on such conversations to decipher what is going on.

The first things you learn when you start asking questions is that the organization has certain values that are supposed to create an image of the organization. In Figure 2.1, these are shown as the organization's "espoused values." In DEC, you were told that they believe in teamwork, that you cannot get good decisions without arguing out what everyone's point of view is and obtaining buy-in from those who have to implement decisions. Therefore they had to make it easy for people to communicate with each other. You may even have been told that these values came directly from Ken Olsen, the founder of the company and that at one time in the company's history he had even forbidden having doors on offices. In this company, when they had meetings they tended to be free-for-alls and highly emotional. You may also have been given some documents, pamphlets, or short papers that described the company's values, principles, ethics, and visions and been told that these documents reflected their basic values: integrity, teamwork, customer orientation, product quality, and so on. In Hewlett-Packard new employees were given a little book that describes the "HP Way."

In Ciba-Geigy, you were told that good decisions cannot be made without careful thought and that they value privacy and the opportunity for employees to really think things through before going into action. You would have heard that this approach was necessary because the nature of their technology was such that careful individual research and thought was the only way to reach a good decision. In this company, meetings were formal and consisted mainly of senior people announcing the decisions made and what now had to be implemented by junior people.

In Ciba-Geigy, you would also have been given various documents that purported to describe the company's values and principles. But to your surprise, many of the points on the list of values would be almost identical to the ones that DEC gave you. Ciba-Geigy was also customer-oriented, cared about teamwork, product quality, integrity, and so on. How could two organizations that espoused so many of the same values have completely different physical layouts and working styles? You also may have noticed that some of the values mentioned did not seem to fit the observed behavior. For example, both organizations espoused teamwork as a value, but both were highly individualistic, encouraged competitive behavior among their employees, and had reward systems that were geared entirely to the individual.

Having read a lot about culture in the popular press, you are now tempted to guess that these two organizations can be fitted into a "typology." Clearly, Ciba-Geigy seemed to have been a "command-and-control" kind of organization, while DEC seemed to have been a flatter, network kind of organization in which people felt personally empowered. You may also have had emotional reactions to these labels, based on your own past experience and values. So now you have to dig still deeper to reconcile the inconsistencies that you have observed and been told about.

The longer you hang around and the more questions you ask, the more you see obvious inconsistencies between some of the espoused values and the visible behavior. For example, both companies espoused customer orientation, yet neither was producing products that were particularly easy to understand or use, and neither had people who seemed very polite or service-oriented.

What these inconsistencies tell you is that a deeper level of thought and perception is driving the overt behavior. The deeper level may or may not be consistent with the values and principles that are espoused by the organization. If you are to understand the culture, you must decipher what is going on at this deeper level.

Level Three: Shared Tacit Assumptions

To understand this deeper level, you have to think historically about these organizations. Throughout the history of the company, what were the values, beliefs, and assumptions of the founders and key leaders that made it successful? Recall that organizations are started by individuals or small teams who initially impose their own beliefs, values, and assumptions on the people whom they hire. If the founders' values and assumptions are out of line with what the environment of the organization allows or affords, the organization fails and never develops a culture in the first place. But suppose, for example, that Ken Olsen, the founder of DEC, believed that to obtain good decisions and implementation of those decisions, people must argue things out and get buy-in on all decisions, and that the imposition of this way of working created a set of products that were successful. He then could attract and retain others who believed the same thing (that one must always argue things out). If by this means they continued to be successful in creating products and services that the market liked, these beliefs and values would gradually come to be shared and taken for granted. They become tacit assumptions about the nature of the world and how to succeed in it.

And as DEC continued to succeed and grow, these assumptions grew stronger.

In analyzing DEC's culture you would observe two other factors. Ken Olsen was an American and an electrical engineer who grew up in the academic environment of MIT's Lincoln Labs. Many of the values and assumptions he brought to the table reflected U.S. values, academic norms of open debate, and the technological realities of electrical engineering and computer design. No one knew what was possible in interactive computing, so strong debate was a far better problem-solving method than arbitrary authority. Experimentation and internal competition were appropriate to the development of a new technology.

In Ciba-Geigy, the founders were Swiss-German chemists working on dyestuffs and agricultural chemicals. Unlike electrical engineering, chemistry is a much more hierarchical science in which experiments have to be very carefully done because of the dangers of mistakes. Individual creative thought was as or more relevant than group debates, and researchers with more knowledge and experience were more valued and trusted. A highly disciplined organization that could efficiently implement solutions would attract people who liked discipline and order, and as they succeeded, they also came to take it for granted that hierarchy, discipline, and order were the only way to run an effective organization based on chemistry and basic research. In either case, then, one could "explain" the essence of the culture if one understood national background, core technology underlying the business, and the personalities of the founders.

The essence of culture is then the jointly learned values and beliefs that work so well that they become taken for granted and non-negotiable. At this point they come to function more as tacit assumptions that become shared and taken for granted as the organization continues to be successful. It is important to remember that these assumptions resulted from a joint learning process. Originally, they were just in the heads of founders and leaders. They became shared and taken for granted only as the new members of the organization realized that the beliefs, values, and assumptions of their founders led to organizational success and so must be "right."

Recall the stories from Chapter One. The new CEO of Atari did not understand the tacit assumption that products (computers and video games) result from a group effort. The IT manager introducing the paperless office at Acme Insurance did not understand the tacit assumption that getting one's normal work finished always had priority over training and that short-run productivity goals were always more important than long-range productivity improvements. The P&G change team did understand that the unionized plants would not adopt a new method until they had developed trust in management and that the culture of these plants had been built up over decades on the tacit assumption that management could not be trusted; they would first have to evolve to a new assumption and show that the new production system would actually benefit the unionized workers.

So, How Do We Define Culture?

Culture is a pattern of shared tacit assumptions that was learned by a group as it solved its problems of external adaptation and internal integration, that has worked well enough to be considered valid and, therefore, to be taught to new members as the correct way to perceive, think, and feel in relation to those problems.

What really drives daily behavior is the learned, shared, tacit assumptions on which people base their view of reality—as it is and as it should be. It results in what is popularly thought of as "the way we do things around here," but even the employees in the organization cannot, without help, reconstruct the underlying assumptions on which their daily behavior rests. They know only that this is the way, and they count on it. Life becomes predictable and meaningful. If you understand those assumptions, it is easy to see how they lead to the kind of behavioral artifacts that you observe. But doing the reverse is very difficult; you cannot infer the assumptions just from observing the behavior. If you really want to understand the culture, you must have a process involving systematic observation and talking to insiders to help make the tacit assumptions explicit (see Chapter Four).

Implications of This Definition

The implications of this way of thinking about culture are profound. For one thing, you begin to realize that culture is so stable and difficult to change because it represents the accumulated learning of a group—the ways of thinking, feeling, and perceiving the world that have made the group successful. For another thing, you realize that the important parts of culture are essentially invisible. Members of the organization cannot readily tell you what their culture is, any more than fish, if they could talk, could tell you what water is. And this point is crucial to our understanding of why cultures cannot be "measured" and "quantified" through surveys or other techniques that only ask about behavior and espoused values.

Furthermore, you begin to realize that there is no right or wrong culture, no better or worse culture, except in relation to what the organization is trying to do and what the environment in which it is operating allows. General arguments of the sort you read in popular literature—about becoming more team-based, or creating a learning organization, or empowering employees—are all invalid unless they show how the tacit assumptions on which these "new values" are based are adaptive to the environment in which the organization has to function. In some markets and with some technologies, teamwork and employee empowerment are essential and the only way the organization can continue to succeed. In other market environments or with other technologies, tight discipline and highly structured relationships are the prerequisites to success. There is no best or right culture, as the evolution and ultimate demise of DEC illustrated.

Another important implication of this definition is that culture is a "pattern" of assumptions that are interconnected to varying degrees. It is very tempting to look for one or two key assumptions and then to label the culture on that basis, as one could do by calling DEC a "networked culture" and Ciba-Geigy a "command-and-control culture." As we will see below, the label makes it easy to miss other dimensions that are just as important to understanding the culture; hence a culture description should always be a multi-dimensional diagram. The multi-dimensionality becomes especially important when assessing the strengths and "weaknesses" of a culture. When a dimension is identified that has become dysfunctional and needs to be changed, one also has to understand how the functional elements must be preserved and how they can actually aid the change process.

The Complexity of Culture: Digital Equipment Corporation

The DEC culture can be represented by two diagrams that illustrate not only the number of dimensions that have to be taken into account but also their interconnection (see Figures 2.2 and 2.3). The purpose of showing these diagrams and analyzing the DEC culture in some detail is to illustrate the complexity of a culture. In practice, it would take a long period of living in the organization to be able to depict the tacit assumptions in this level of detail. I was able to create these diagrams because I had consulted with DEC for over twenty-five years. For most purposes, this level of detail is not necessary, as we will see.

When DEC started, it was, in effect, helping to create the computer market. No one knew for sure what the right products

Figure 2.2. DEC's Cultural Paradigm: Part I

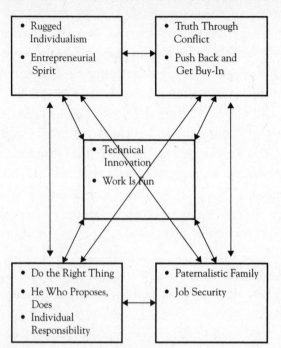

© Schein, E.H. *DEC Is Dead, Long Live DEC: The Lasting Legacy of Digital Equipment Corporation*. Berrett-Koehler, 2003.

were and what customers would want in the long run. The ten deep assumptions on which DEC was built were that:

- Rugged individualism and an entrepreneurial spirit in the employees are the only way to succeed.
- Employees are willing and able to take responsibility.
- Smart entrepreneurial people who are creating innovations must debate things out to arrive at "truth."
- Work must be fun.
- Everyone is a member of the family and, therefore, has job security.
- Customers must be treated with total respect, must always be told the truth.
- Responsible people with goodwill can solve any problem.

Figure 2.3. DEC's Cultural Paradigm: Part II

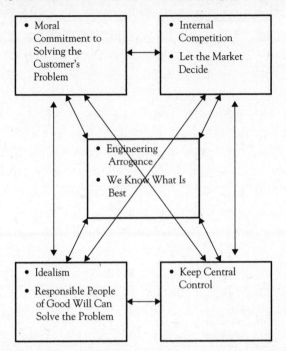

© Schein, E.H. *DEC Is Dead, Long Live DEC: The Lasting Legacy of Digital Equipment Corporation.* Berrett-Koehler, 2003.

- Engineers know best (especially when most early customers are also engineers and techies).
- Internal competition among projects and letting the market decide what wins is the best way to define priorities.
- Maintaining centralized paternalistic control is essential.

In describing and analyzing a culture, it is important to recognize that some of these assumptions interact directly with others. One cannot have strong debates without responsible people and one cannot sustain the emotionally draining emphasis on debate and pushback without the security of the paternalistic climate. Failure only meant that the person was in the wrong job and could move to another job and succeed. It is also possible for assumptions to conflict with each other, in which case one must identify which assumption has priority in cases of conflict.

For example, the assumption that people can be given and can exercise responsibility is potentially in conflict with the assumption that one must maintain centralized control. When DEC was young and small, these two assumptions could co-exist, but when DEC was older, larger, and had developed strong autonomous engineering managers, these managers overrode many of Ken Olsen's efforts to maintain centralized control.

These assumptions working in concert with each other created an incredible sense of empowerment at all levels of the organization and an atmosphere of involvement and commitment that created a highly successful company. With success, the assumptions became taken for granted as "the way we do things." But reaching consensus by this means was a slow and often painful process. Successful negotiation and buy-in depended very much on the trust that developed in the "family," which was based on the members' being familiar with one another's styles. If the hardware developer asked a software counterpart whether the software would be ready in six months and received an affirmative answer, he would know whether this meant literally six months, or maybe nine months, or maybe not at all unless he kept pressuring his associate. Engineers and managers were "functionally familiar" with each other. They knew how to calibrate each other from working closely together over some period of time.

If a decision was made and down the road someone questioned it, it was his or her obligation to "push back" and "do the right thing" (as the deep assumptions put it). This process often unraveled decisions and improved them, but it took much longer and only worked if the functional familiarity among the players was high and they could trust each other not to bring up trivial issues. This model of how to work with each other was enormously successful and catapulted DEC into the Fortune 50.

But success brought growth, and as the organization grew, the debate was increasingly with strangers rather than trusted colleagues. Functional familiarity became rare and was replaced with formal contracts, checking on each other, and playing power games to make things happen. At the same time, the technology itself became more complex; this required a shift from an environment in which individual engineers designed complete products to one of large teams of engineers having to coordinate their efforts to build the complex products that were becoming possible and desirable. The highly individualistic, competitive, creative engineers found themselves increasingly having to coordinate their part of the design with others whose ideas they did not necessarily respect. The sense of involvement and commitment that characterized small projects was hard to sustain on large projects with multiple parts that had to be coordinated in a disciplined fashion. Whereas early in its history DEC engineers were kings and dominated decisions, as the business matured other functions such as finance and marketing became more powerful; the result was growing conflicts among functional groups that had created their own subcultures over time.

DEC's success attracted competitors, and as computers increasingly became a commodity, time-to-market and the cost of development and production became major factors. These external forces made the original assumptions about individual autonomy and empowerment increasingly dysfunctional. The empowered engineering managers became powerful. Not only could they not agree among themselves, but they also ignored or overruled Ken Olsen's efforts to focus because they now felt more powerful than their founder. DEC leadership recognized these new forces and talked about shifting to smaller units in which the original assumptions that people believed in could be implemented, and would allow focusing on a smaller number of products, more discipline and hierarchy. But leadership could not give up the tacit assumptions of individual empowerment and debate because that was the basis of their success as innovators. As they grew, they became increasingly victim to a political process in which baronies grew and mistrust replaced the functional familiarity on which the culture had depended.

Central control became ever more difficult. Excessive costs, slow time-to-market, and inability to develop a coherent strategy in an increasingly complex market caused serious financial problems, until finally in the 1990s DEC had a major change in leadership and embraced a more hierarchical structure that would allow the discipline and efficiency the market now needed. As this happened, DEC old-timers lamented what they regarded as a loss of the DEC culture and many of them left voluntarily to build organizations of their own on the DEC cultural model. Paradoxically, even as DEC the economic entity disappeared, the DEC culture survived in its alumni.

The lesson is that a good or right culture is a function of the degree to which shared tacit assumptions create the kind of strategy that is functional in the organization's environment. If you were the kind of person who preferred the open, confrontational type of organization that DEC represented and went to work there in the 1970s, you would have had a blast. If you were there with the same mind-set in the 1990s, you might have found yourself bored by all the rules or out of a job.

The Bottom Line

It is clear that culture is a complex concept that must be analyzed at every level before it can be understood. The biggest risk in working with culture is to oversimplify it and miss several basic facets that matter:

1. Culture is *deep*. If you treat it as a superficial phenomenon, if you assume that you can manipulate it and change it at will, you are sure to fail. Furthermore, culture controls you more than you control culture. You want it that way, because culture gives meaning and predictability to your daily life. As you learn what works, you develop beliefs and assumptions that eventually drop out of awareness and become tacit rules of how to do things, how to think about things, and how to feel.

2. Culture is *broad*. As a group learns to survive in its environment, it learns about all aspects of its external and internal relationships. Beliefs and assumptions form about daily life, how to get along with the boss, what kind of attitude one should have toward customers, the nature of one's career in the organization, what it takes to get ahead, what the sacred cows are, and so on. Deciphering culture can therefore be an endless task. If you do not have a specific focus or reason for wanting to understand your organizational culture, you will find it boundless and frustrating.

3. Culture is *stable*. The members of a group want to hold on to their cultural assumptions because culture provides meaning and makes life predictable. Humans do not like chaotic, unpredictable situations and work hard to stabilize and "normalize" them. Any prospective culture change therefore launches massive amounts of anxiety and resistance to change. If you want to change some elements of your culture, you must recognize that you are tackling some of the most stable parts of your organization.

Questions for the Reader

So what should you do differently tomorrow?

- Take some time to reflect on your own concept of culture and to integrate into it some of the insights from this chapter.

- Think about the organization in which you work, and see whether you can come up with some of its espoused values. Does the organization live its espoused values? If not, what are the deeper, shared tacit assumptions that explain daily behavior.

- Start by thinking about the artifacts around you and the behavior you observe. Locate things that puzzle you; ask an old-timer why they are that way. Try to see the culture as an outsider might (but for now, try not to evaluate it or think about changing it).

3

WHAT ARE THE ELEMENTS AND DIMENSIONS OF ORGANIZATIONAL CULTURE?

The Popular View: Inventories and Typologies

When you think about culture, chances are you identify some aspect of how the people in your organization relate to each other and how they do their jobs—"the way we do things around here." The most common view is that culture is about human relations in the organization. Culture is often confused with "climate," how the organization feels, what the employee morale is, how well people are getting along. There is a strong temptation to look for broad categories such as "command and control" or "autocratic versus democratic." Culture typologies built on these popular views talk about levels of "sociability" and "solidarity" or about "internal versus external focus" and "flexibility versus stability and control."[1] Almost all of these typologies and the questionnaires designed to measure the underlying dimensions are based on some aspect of the human relations inside the organization or in connection with the environment. When culture change is proposed it is almost always in relation to more teamwork, employee involvement, reducing the layers of supervision in the organization, creating lateral communication, building loyalty and commitment in the organization, empowering employees, and becoming more customer oriented. Most questionnaires that purport to assess culture deal with these same issues.

These views of culture are correct but dangerously narrow. Cultural assumptions in organizations do grow around how people in the organization relate to each other, but that is only a fraction of what culture covers. Culture-change programs that focus narrowly on how employees currently perceive their organization versus how they would like the organization to be are unlikely to work because they ignore other elements of culture that are more deeply embedded and may not even be noticed.

For example, a large insurance company hired a new CEO who concluded that among the company's main problems was a lack of innovation. He launched multiple programs to increase innovation, all of which failed. Why? A number of employee focus groups were launched to analyze the problem. In reviewing the company's history it was revealed that past success was based on a tightly structured system of figuring out the best solution to any given problem, documenting the solution, putting all of the solutions into large manuals organized by every conceivable kind of problem that could arise, and systematically rewarding employees for using the rules written out in the manuals.

Over the years, employees had learned that the road to success was to apply the rules. The number of manuals grew to cover every new situation that arose. Employees who did not like to work in this kind of rule-bound, structured environment were encouraged to leave the organization, leading to a workforce that was comfortable in the structured environment. Previous CEOs had glorified this system of working, and indeed it had been highly successful in building the company. It came to be taken for granted that the best way to work was to follow the rules in the manuals.

The new CEO saw that the company was in a changing environment and realized that many of the new situations the company would face could not be preprogrammed. Employees would have to learn to think for themselves as they faced a turbulent environment. He launched various campaigns to reward innovation (suggestion boxes, prizes for new ideas) yet received little response. He did not realize that the entire organization was built on the assumption that the correct way to do things was to follow the rules, and that over the years this assumption had become deeply embedded in all the layers of management and employees because it was successful. It was in the very fabric of how the organization operated, built into how the company recruited, rewarded, and promoted people. For this organization to change its way of working would require a complete assessment of all aspects of its culture. Ironically, if this CEO became aware of these deep cultural elements, perhaps he could have succeeded by imposing a new rule. Every month every department had to invent three new ways of doing things and write up a manual to that effect!!!

If a cultural assessment is to be done, what content areas would such an assessment have to cover If we look back at the culture diagrams of DEC, we see that many of the tacit assumptions are about people relationships, but what would be missed if we had not looked more deeply into the DEC culture would be the assumption that truth can only be derived by full and open debate and that the mission of the organization was innovation based on good creative engineering. The human relations assumptions were derivative from the assumptions about the mission of the organization and how to best accomplish it.

To give you a more realistic view of what culture covers, look at Exhibit 3.1. It outlines the areas in which cultural assumptions make a difference. The first thing to notice is that cultural assumptions involve not only the internal workings of the organization but, more important, how the organization views itself in relation to its various environments.

Exhibit 3.1. What Is Culture About?

External Survival Issues

- Mission, strategy, goals
- Means: structure, systems, processes
- Measurement: error-detection and correction systems

(Continued)

Internal Integration Issues

- Common language and concepts
- Group boundaries and identity
- The nature of authority and relationships
- Allocation of rewards and status

Deeper Underlying Assumptions

- Human relationships to nature
- The nature of reality and truth
- The nature of human nature
- The nature of human relationships
- The nature of time and space
- The unknowable and uncontrollable

Culture Content, Part One: Surviving in the External Environment

Mission, Strategy, Goals

To survive and grow, every organization must develop viable assumptions about what to do and how to do it. For an organization to succeed in the sense of accomplishing its mission, surviving, and growing, it must fulfill what its various environments demand and afford. Most organizations evolve assumptions about their basic mission and identity, about their strategic intent, financial policies, fundamental way of organizing themselves and their work, way of measuring themselves, and means for correcting themselves when they are perceived to be off target.

When the organization was first created, its founders and early leaders had a strong sense of mission and identity—what they were trying to be, what product or market they were trying to develop, who they were and what justified them. To raise money, they had to develop a credible story around these questions, and the first set of employees needed to buy into and believe the story, even if they knew initially that it was a risk and might not work out. But if it did work out and the organization succeeded, the founders and the employees would begin to form shared assumptions around those initial beliefs—and over time come to take them for granted. The deep sense of mission and identity may become so taken for granted that it surfaces only if some event violates it and thereby brings it to consciousness.

An example from the Swiss company Ciba-Geigy illustrates the point. In the mid-1970s, C-G consisted of four major product divisions (dyestuffs, industrial chemicals, agricultural chemicals, and pharmaceuticals) and many country units. Historically the company traced its roots to the dyestuffs business and the important discoveries made in the R&D labs that led to new products in the agricultural and pharmaceutical domains. The company recognized that its strength was in R&D and that it had remained profitable largely because of patent protection. Leadership recognized that, as patents expired and competition in each market grew, C-G needed to improve marketing and reduce costs.

Thus far, this story may seem like fairly traditional evolution; so where does culture come in? To improve marketing skills, C-G empowered its U.S. subsidiary to purchase a consumer goods company because organizations of that kind learn how to do sophisticated marketing. They purchased Airwick, a maker of air fresheners, carpet cleaners, and other products to remove unpleasant odors. For a number of years, Airwick struggled along but gradually became profitable, not only in the United States but in various European countries where it developed subsidiaries.

At that time, I was working with the C-G corporate executive committee in running an annual meeting of its top fifty functional, divisional, and country managers. In one of these meetings, the president of the U.S. subsidiary was reporting on the progress of Airwick and showing videotape of a particularly successful advertising campaign that introduced a new product, Carpet Fresh.

The ads showed a housewife sprinkling Carpet Fresh powder on her rugs and a minute or so later vacuuming it up, to illustrate how easy the product was to use.

I was sitting next to a member of the executive committee, a man who had developed several of C-G's major chemical products and who saw himself as an important strategist in the company. Watching the videotape, he began to squirm in his seat, showed signs of great tension, and finally leaned over to me and said in a loud whisper, "You know, Schein, those aren't even *products*."

In that moment, I glimpsed his image of what C-G was all about. He saw it as a company producing "important products" that combated starvation (industrial pesticides enabled third-world countries to grow crops) and saved lives (pharmaceutical products were geared to curing major diseases). In that context, and with that sense of mission, how could one possibly view an air or carpet freshener as worthy of being called a "product"? How could one possibly want to associate with such a trivial matter? This man's self-image was violated by C-G's association with Airwick—never mind that the whole idea was to learn something about marketing and that Airwick was beginning to show good financial results. Airwick just did not fit.

Some months later, I learned of another way in which this aspect of the corporate culture impacted their daily functioning. The European division of Airwick was based in Paris, and that office hired a very talented woman to be chief financial officer. They reported with pride that they were beginning to break the gender barrier in their promotional policies, and she was a prime example. However, she left some months later and related the following incident. In organizing Airwick's European operation, she needed a more efficient and speedier accounting system than what C-G was using. She went to the corporate head of accounting in the Basel headquarters and requested permission and funds to institute the new system, only to be told, "Mrs. Smith, I think you will find that our accounting system has been quite adequate to the task for one hundred years or so, and it should certainly be adequate, therefore, to your tasks." Needless to say, she left and Airwick managers were forced to bootleg systems in secrecy that would meet their needs.

The cultural moral of this story is that an acquisition strategy has to fit the existing culture. Even though the purpose of the acquisition was to learn marketing from a consumer-goods company, this particular set of products was giving C-G cultural indigestion. C-G's sense of mission and self-image were violated by these "non-products," even though Airwick was beginning to show profit in many countries. To deal with their discomfort, the executive committee appointed a senior Swiss manager to evaluate the future of Airwick over a period of several years and recommend what C-G should do with it. From a cultural perspective, it was obvious that he would eventually recommend that they sell Airwick—which is what they did. At the same time they reaffirmed their self-image of only making acquisitions of companies that were based on sophisticated technology. At subsequent annual meetings, it was stated explicitly that C-G should only buy companies with a strong technical base. Culture was driving the acquisition strategy.

C-G managers may or may not have recognized that they were dealing with culture, and that they held deeply embedded assumptions about who they were, what kinds of things qualified as products, and what acquisition strategy was OK or not OK. We tend to think that we can separate strategy from culture, but we fail to notice that in most organizations strategic thinking is deeply colored by tacit assumptions about who they are and what their mission is.

Over its history, any organization learns a great deal about what kinds of strategies work and what ones do not. Such strategies are about types of products and services, types of markets, level of quality desired, level of price that the customer base will accept, and so on. These points are reflected in the first category in Exhibit 3.1: the basic mission of the organization, its strategic intent, and the goals derived from the mission and strategy.

This category of culture is so central that it warrants another example to illustrate how these culture dynamics work.

Early in the history of Digital Equipment (DEC), the mission was to bring efficient interactive computing to the scientifically minded user, offer distributed computing power to organizations, and show the world the power of a midsized computer. Its product strategy, concept of who the customer was, pricing, and decisions about level of quality all were driven during the company's high-growth phase by these strategic goals. The degree to which they came to be taken for granted and thus part of the culture at DEC could be measured by the difficulty the company had in designing a product to compete with IBM's personal computer. At some level, DEC engineers did not really respect the "dumb user" for whom a low-cost, user-friendly PC would have to be designed, inasmuch as all of their past success had been with sophisticated users who were perfectly willing to do some of their own programming. The high technical standards and quality of DEC products also made them more elegant than they needed to be and more expensive, hence not very competitive in the new PC market.

Several cultural forces conspired to make the DEC entry into the PC world a basic failure. First was the deep assumption that the engineers basically did not care much about the dumb user. Second, smart people should be empowered to do the right thing. Three engineering managers with very strong ideas about the PC proposed potential products, named the DECmate, the Pro, and the Rainbow. At this point in its history, DEC was already fairly large and differentiated, and the engineering managers all had their own power bases and strong convictions that their products would win in the marketplace. They were themselves products of the DEC culture.

A third cultural assumption that came into play was that, if one could not make a clear internal decision, "Let the marketplace decide." A tradition had grown up in the company that having internally competing groups was healthy; the marketplace would reveal which was the best product. DEC had been successful with this internal-competition approach and hence did not question it. It was OK to have three competing PC projects.

But the cultural assumption that each manager and employee was obliged to "do the right thing" led to another problem. Ken Olsen, the founder, and other managers believed that the three proposed products were over-engineered, too elegant, and too expensive. Yet no one, not even Olsen, could convince the engineering managers to scale down their products. In the DEC culture, one could not order the three groups to do things differently; one could only try to convince them. In the end, all three products failed competitively, even though each claimed to be an excellent PC. The story highlights how a strategic failure in the product-development arena can only be understood in the context of culture.

Questions for the Reader

Ask yourself and others in your organization these questions:

- What is the fundamental mission of your organization? What is its reason for being? What justifies its existence in the larger scheme of things?

- How do your organization's strategy and the goals derived from it fit that mission?

- Where did this strategy and set of goals come from? Is the strategy completely based on formal reasoning and logic, or is it partly a product of the beliefs and biases of the organization's founders and leaders?

Means: Structure, Systems, and Processes

How an organization decides to implement its strategy and goals is the next level of culture content. The formal organizational structure in one company may be very tall, steep, and multilayered;

if they succeed with this structure, they come to believe that it is the correct way to organize. In another organization, the founder creates a flat structure with many overlapping committees and task forces; here too, if they succeed they believe just as strongly that theirs is the correct way to organize. The degree to which the structure is adapted to the task to be performed and the nature of the environment in which the organization operates creates the shared tacit assumptions about how to organize. Glib labeling of an organization as a command-and-control type or a flat-network type reflects some elements of this category, but note that such labels describe only one small aspect of the corporate culture—and often a very irrelevant aspect.

The insurance company CEO in the earlier example in this chapter did not realize that the compulsive adherence to rules was based on evolving ways of working that fitted the early strategy of the company and was, therefore, thoroughly imbedded. Simply calling for innovation would not overcome employee desire to stick to routines that had worked very well in the past.

The complexity of cultural analysis is also revealed in this category in that an organization can have a shared mission and strategic intent, yet units may organize themselves differently in their efforts to achieve it. Subcultures are thus created within the organization's overall culture. As organizations grow and differentiate themselves into functional, product, market, and geographically based units, they also develop subcultures around each of these bases. Such subcultures may have learned to be very different from each other because the parts of the organization have to succeed in different kinds of environments.

For example, in the 1960s a large aerospace company, Northrop, prided itself on its egalitarian structure; there were few levels and few rules throughout its production units. During a workshop to analyze their culture, a group of senior managers could not figure out why Northrop's headquarters organization in Los Angeles seemed to violate this culture by being multilayered, very rigid, and very status conscious. There were three levels of dining rooms, all kinds of rules about dress and demeanor, rigid adherence to hours of work, and so on. They finally realized that the subculture of the headquarters organization had developed this way because its primary customer was the Pentagon. The military visitors to the company were used to a system in which status, dress codes, rank, privileges, and so on were all very well defined.

In their factories, a completely different set of assumptions grew up around the complex technology, which required a high degree of teamwork and mutual trust among employees. The nature of the work defined the rules and norms in terms of quality of work and getting the job done. There were no time clocks; hours were determined by the nature of the task; the selection and promotion system encouraged hiring of relatives because it was easier to develop trusting relationships in a family atmosphere; and status was determined by knowledge and skill level, not by formal title. Once the group recognized that the tasks of factory and headquarters differed, they realized that it was appropriate for these units to develop distinct subcultures.

Recall from Chapter One how Procter & Gamble restructured the manufacturing division into a set of autonomously self-managed plants to achieve the shared strategic intent of becoming a low-cost producer while maintaining high quality. In their marketing, sales, and financial divisions, no such structures emerged, showing that different means of accomplishing a shared strategy can coexist. Similarly, within DEC's very egalitarian environment, there existed a service organization that was highly structured, authoritarian, and disciplined because in the service environment only such a structure could deliver efficiently what the customers required.

Every organization that succeeds develops a way of structuring work; defining the production and marketing processes; and creating the kinds of information, reward, and control systems it needs to operate effectively. As these systems continue to work, they are taken for granted as the way to do things, and an employee who moves from one unit to another often finds it difficult to learn how to work in the new environment. It is for this reason that, once organizations have strong cultures, they prefer to promote from within. It is often too difficult to train an outsider in "how things are done around here." On the other hand, if the way things are done becomes dysfunctional in a changing environment, it is these elements of the culture that are often the hardest to change because people have been hired, been trained, and become habituated to this way of doing things. As we will see, this issue became critical in the ultimate economic demise of DEC.

Questions for the Reader

Ask yourself and others:

- How did your own organization develop its approach to meeting goals?
- How and why did it develop the kind of structure that it has? Do the formal structure and the design of how work gets done largely reflect the beliefs of the founders and leaders of the organization?
- To what extent are the means used in the functional and geographic divisions the same (or different)?
- Is there evidence that your organization has strong subcultures within it? What are they based on?

Measurement: Error-Detection and Correction Systems

The third cultural issue seen in Exhibit 3.1 concerns how the organization measures itself, detects errors, and corrects them. Organizations evolve different mechanisms for deciphering the environment: financial indicators, frequent debriefing of the sales force to determine what is going on "out there," formal marketing surveys, creating special departments whose job it is to find out what is going on and bring the information into the organization, rates of employee turnover, morale and other kinds of surveys, and so on. The CEO, the sales force, the purchasing department, the R&D unit, the personnel function, and the marketing department all have windows to the environment, but every company develops its own ways of using them and, if successful, comes to believe that theirs are the correct ways.

For most business organizations, financial performance is the primary error-detecting mechanism because of its seeming objectivity, but cultural assumptions dominate even what kind of information is gathered and how it is interpreted. For example, some companies go almost exclusively by the stock price as the indicator of how they are doing. Others look at debt-to-equity ratios, cash flow, or market share. In each case, cultural assumptions arise from the indicators that work best. If the organization is functionally organized, it may also develop a subculture around the finance function, and actual conflicts may develop between finance, production, engineering, and marketing over which indicators to use in assessing company performance.

What is defined as a significant variance or an error itself varies from company to company and becomes embedded in cultural assumptions. One story about Levi Strauss has it that they were able to make major changes by declaring a crisis whenever the profitability index dropped by 0.5 percent. What is culturally significant in this story is not that they responded to such a small variance but that employees accepted management's definition that this was indeed a crisis.

Error correction, like error detection, reflects the history of the company and the personalities of its founders. Many organizations develop what has come to be labeled a "blaming culture." Managers tend to be trained to think in terms of simple cause-and-effect; they need to feel in control, and the broader managerial culture makes a sacred cow out of individual accountability. Given this way of thinking, if things go wrong the obvious response is to find out who is to blame, who is responsible, who is accountable.

But companies differ markedly in how they respond to what they find out. In some organizations, once blamed, a person is instantly dismissed. In other organizations, particularly those having grown around strong paternalistic and lifetime-employment values, this person may not even be told that he or she has been blamed but is simply taken off the fast-track career ladder, given less-important assignments, and in other ways punished by having career opportunities permanently limited.

A third pattern that was evident in DEC was to be "put into the penalty box." Since everyone belonged to the family, no one could lose membership (a job), but you could lose your assignment on a project and be forced to find another assignment on your own. If you found another job in the company and did well in it, you were celebrated as a case of successful "rehabilitation." Underlying this system was an important assumption about people: if someone fails, it is because of a mismatch between the person and the job; the person is always OK, but the person-job match may not be. This assumption made it clear how much people were valued, but it also made it clear that everyone had a great responsibility to manage his or her own career and to speak up if there was a mismatch.

A fourth system of error correction used by many organizations attempts to avoid personal blame, instead seeking the root or systemic cause of the failure. The U.S. Army's program of "after action reviews," project postmortems, and other kinds of reviews attempts to build more learning into the process instead of blame. Note, though, that such systemic reviews do not work if the culture is strongly individualistic and competitive because people will not open up negative information about themselves and each other. If the organization develops a blaming culture, employees disassociate themselves from a failed project as quickly as possible and are reluctant to engage in a postmortem because it might reveal that they are in some way to blame. Only if enough trust and teamwork are built up over time, and only if that way of working succeeds, does systemic error analysis and correction work and become acceptable.

A current example illustrating the complexity of measurement is the issue of safety—protecting both the public and employees in industries that are hazardous. The Alpha Power Company that supplies power to a large metropolitan area is strategically dedicated to providing reliable service safely. Because of the inherent danger in managing this technology, not only do employees sometimes get hurt severely, but the public is also at risk from explosions, stray voltage, and other hazards deriving from the delivery of this service. The measurement of reliability (keeping the power on) competes with the measurement of number of injuries to employees or the public (shutting down power temporarily when a hazard has been discovered). Cultural norms gradually develop around levels of "acceptable risk," priorities of what to maintain

---

Questions for the Reader

Ask yourself and others:

- What are the error-detection systems in your organization? How do you discover that you are not meeting goals and targets?

- What do you do about it if you discover that some important goals are not being met?

- Are there variations among parts of the organization in how they measure themselves and what they do about the results? Can you see evidence in such variation of important subculture differences?

when, how much money to spend on aging equipment, and what target numbers to shoot for on rates of employee injuries. The culture begins to reflect systems of how to make compromises, how to set priorities, and how to keep searching for even better measures of how the safety programs are doing.

I have tried to show in these last few pages that culture is heavily implicated in the basic mission, strategy, means, measurement, and remedial systems of the organization. Culture is not just about people and how we manage them. It is not just about teamwork or reward systems. Cultural assumptions develop over time regarding the core fabric of the organization and its basic mission and strategy. If you fail to take these parts of the culture into account when trying to change other parts of the culture, you will discover that the other parts do not respond as you hope they will.

Culture Content, Part Two: Integrating the Human Organization

The popularized view of culture focuses on the relationships among the people in the organization, the incentive and reward systems, and the degree of teamwork, superior-subordinate relationships, communication, and all the other processes that make the workplace more or less productive and pleasant. The cultural assumptions that grow up around these areas are, of course, critical. But they interact with the externally oriented assumptions we have reviewed (and listed in the first part of Exhibit 3.1) and thus cannot be treated in isolation.

Common Language and Concepts

The most obvious manifestations of culture are common language and common ways of thinking. We see this most clearly at the national level, when we travel and find out how difficult it is to get along in other countries if we do not know the language or how the locals think. On a trip to southern France many years ago, I found myself in a small rural post office in a line waiting to buy some stamps. Just as it was my turn, a man came into the post office and started to talk to the clerk, interrupting my hesitant French request. To my surprise, the clerk turned her attention to the man and dealt with his issue for several minutes before returning to my request. When I told this story later to my French friends, they laughed and said: "You know, Ed, the situation is even worse than you imagine. The clerk was going by the cultural principle that she will deal with whoever's agenda she considers most important. By your letting the intruder capture her attention, you were displaying to the entire post office your low sense of self-esteem." Evidently what I should have done was to loudly and firmly recapture the clerk's attention instead of standing by in silent resentment.

The organizational equivalent of such events occurs when new employees try to figure out how to dress, how to talk to their bosses, how to behave in group meetings, how to decipher all the jargon and acronyms that other employees throw around, how assertive to be, how late to stay at work, and so on. One reason it takes time before one can become productive in a new organization is because so many of the norms, ways of working, and ways of thinking are unique to that organization and have to be learned by trial and error.

For example, in DEC "real work" was defined as debating things out with others and getting buy-in, whereas in Ciba-Geigy real work meant thinking things out by oneself. At one point in DEC history, management decided they needed to speed up the process of cultural learning, so they launched a series of what they called "boot camps" for new employees in which newcomers and old-timers were taken off-site to spend several days with a facilitator. The boot camp provided opportunities for the old-timers to talk about the DEC culture and for newcomers to ask questions about all the things puzzling them in their new work environment.

Questions for the Reader

Ask yourself and others:

- Does your organization use special jargon or acronyms that you take for granted but that an outsider finds strange and undecipherable? What are some examples?
- What do your friends notice about your language and way of thinking that they associate with membership in your organization?
- If you have worked for more than one organization, what are the differences among them in how people talk and think?

Group Boundaries: Who Is In and Who Is Out?

Every organization develops ways of identifying degrees of membership, ranging from uniforms and badges to more subtle indicators such as who gets what parking slots, stock options, and other perquisites. As newcomers learn the language and ways of thinking, they find they are more often included in organizational events. An important stage of acceptance is when the newcomer is trusted enough to be told "secrets," information about what is really going on, who is in and who is out, what the company is really working on, details about the private lives of senior executives, and so on. With such membership comes the obligation to be more loyal, not to reveal those secrets to outsiders, to work harder, and to invest more of oneself in the organization. The shared tacit assumptions about membership and its obligations make up a significant portion of what we think of as the culture of an organization. But once again, remember: it is only one portion of the culture.

Questions for the Reader

Ask yourself and others:

- What are the badges of membership in your organization? Are there uniforms that signify membership?
- Do you use special symbols or privileges to symbolize degrees of membership?
- Do you think about who is an insider, who is an outsider, and what this means in terms of your relationship to those people?
- Can you recall what it was like to enter your current organization?
- Have you brought anyone into your organization? How did you manage the process?

How Relationships, Rank, and Authority Are Defined

Organizations differ in the assumptions they make about authority relationships and the degree of intimacy that is considered appropriate among members. Some organizations are aggressively egalitarian and minimize the psychological distance between bosses and subordinates. A hierarchy may exist, but subordinates are encouraged to use first names with their bosses, go around levels when it seems appropriate, and do the right thing even if it means insubordination (as was the case in DEC). In other organizations, the hierarchy is formally observed, relationships across levels are very formal, and it is inconceivable to go around levels or challenge the boss (as was the case in Ciba-Geigy). Both companies thought of themselves as "families," but for the former the family was a bunch of rebellious adolescents challenging their parents all the time, while for the latter the family was a set of "good" children who always did what their authoritarian parents told them to do.

Closely connected to authority relationships are assumptions about how open and personal relationships should be in the organization. In some organizations, employees are expected to be open about everything—even their feelings toward their bosses and each other. Such organizations are the exception. More common are norms that define clear boundaries about what can and cannot be talked about at work, and what can and cannot be said to the boss or to a subordinate. In some organizations, the assumption is that one leaves one's personal and family life at the door when entering the workplace. I know of a case where an employee's wife committed suicide, yet the employee continued to come to work as if nothing had happened. Others in the organization did not discover his tragedy for six months.

In DEC, people socialized with each other a good deal, especially because of the pattern of two-day off-site "woods meetings" where the work group would be together around the clock. In Ciba-Geigy, certain families got together for dinners, and at the annual meetings there would be one afternoon and evening planned for deliberately letting hair down by having the whole group engage in some novel sport that brought everyone down to the same level of incompetence, followed by an informal dinner. In Silicon Valley, many companies use social events such as parties, ski trips, weekends in San Francisco, and the like as rewards for their employees. In some instances, only the employee team is invited, while in others the spouses are included as well.

The point again is that each organization develops its own cultural assumptions about the degree to which employees are expected to become close to each other. I was told that at Apple people get very close on project teams, but that once the project is finished the friendships don't last. At HP, on the other hand, once friendships are formed they last, even if someone leaves the company.

Questions for the Reader

Ask yourself and others:

- How appropriate is it to interrupt the boss when he or she is speaking?

- If you disagree with the boss, do you feel encouraged or discouraged to voice your disagreement face-to-face? Is it OK to disagree in front of others, or do you have to seek the boss out and disagree privately?

- Does your boss level with you about your performance, or do you have to guess how you are doing?

- If your boss asks you to evaluate him or her, how comfortable would you be saying exactly what you think and feel?

- How would your subordinates answer these questions in regard to you as the boss?

- Can you bring family and personal problems to work, or are you expected to keep them separate from work and private? Do you share with your colleagues or boss the problems you are having at home?

- If you and your partner are in a dual-career situation and you have to go home, say, to tend to a child, do you feel comfortable explaining the situation, or do you feel you have to invent an ironclad excuse to go home (perhaps taking a sick day or vacation day)?

- When you are at an informal event with your colleagues or boss, what kinds of things do you talk about? How comfortable are you in socializing with others in the organization? How many of them are friends whom you see regularly?

Again, keep in mind that there are no right answers. Cultures differ, and any given culture can work under one set of circumstances yet be completely dysfunctional under others.

How Rewards and Status Are Allocated

Every organization develops a reward-and-status system. The most obvious form is pay increases and promotion up the ladder. But organizational cultures differ in the meanings attached to these and other kinds of rewards. In some organizations and for some employees, promotions and monetary rewards such as salary, bonus, stock options, and profit sharing are the primary rewards and sources of status. In other organizations, it is titles that matter, or the number of subordinates who report to you.

What employees care about is often a function of the subculture that they are in, based on occupational background and their "Career Anchor."[2] Sales and marketing employees will care about the kinds of territories they are given, financial employees will care about the support they receive from general management in enforcing their policies and procedures, manufacturing employees will care about the size of their budget for maintenance and purchase of new equipment. Engineers and scientists in the R&D function will care about the size of their project, the project budget, the degree of autonomy with regard to working hours, the visibility they have in the organization, the degree to which senior management consults them about strategic issues, their professional status outside the organization, and opportunities for further learning and development in their area of expertise.

One of the most difficult tasks facing the newcomer in an organization is to decipher the reward-and-status system. What kind of behavior is expected, and how do you know when you are doing the right or wrong thing? What kind of behavior is rewarded, and what kind punished? How do you know when you have been rewarded or punished? One of the most common complaints of employees and managers alike is "I don't know how I'm doing; I don't get any useful feedback." Performance appraisal systems are supposed to provide feedback, but most managers complain that they find it very awkward to be open in talking to their employees about their performance. To deal with this problem, some organizations are experimenting with complex feedback systems, such as "360-degree feedback," in which data are collected from a given employee's boss, peers, and subordinates; amalgamated; and then given back to the employee. But even in these cases, it is surprising how often the person feels he or she cannot really "read" the signals as to whether he or she has been rewarded or punished, or neither. Of course, the degree to which such systems are open depends on the cultural assumptions about the nature of relationships, as we have discussed.

Questions for the Reader

Ask yourself and others:

- In your work situation, what do you consider to be a reward or a punishment?
- What signals do you pay attention to in order to figure out how you are doing?
- When others receive visible rewards, is it clear to you what they did to deserve them? When others are punished, how do you know they are being punished, and is it clear what they did to deserve the punishment?
- Can you identify the people with higher and lower status in your organization, and is it clear to you what their status rests on?

The Bottom Line

Once you answer questions such as these, you have partially deciphered your corporate culture and some of its subcultures. In Chapter Five I will describe a more systematic process to further such deciphering in relation to a problem you are trying to solve.

But even as you gain insight into some elements of your organization's culture and subcultures, you must be aware that you and your organization exist in a larger country culture in which tacit assumptions have grown up about more fundamental issues such as time, space, reality, and human nature. How organizations manage their external survival and internal integration issues is very much correlated with broader assumptions that come into play, especially when organizations become global and need to work with partners or subsidiaries in other countries.

4

DEEPER ASSUMPTIONS

National and Ethnic Bases of Culture

Organizational cultures ultimately are embedded in the national cultures in which an organization operates. Thus the deeper assumptions of the national culture come to be reflected in the organization through the cultural backgrounds of its founders, leaders, and members. For example, Ken Olsen, the founder of DEC, was an American electrical engineer who believed profoundly in the U.S. values of competitive individualism, had a strong moral and ethical sense, and held a deep conviction that people could and should be trusted. These beliefs were reflected in all of the incentive, reward, and control systems that DEC developed. He also believed in individual responsibility and would become upset if he saw managers either failing to take responsibility or abdicating it to others, even if those others were their own superiors. As DEC evolved, it came to mirror in an exaggerated way many of the aspects of U.S. culture.

Similarly, C-G grew up in the Swiss-German context and reflected many of the deep values and assumptions of that part of Switzerland: respect for authority, strong sense of responsibility and obligation to others who know more, loyalty to country and company, and individual autonomy (but combined with a deep belief in collaboration and teamwork). This belief in collaboration was revealed when I was helping to design a workshop for C-G managers and proposed the "NASA Moon Survival" exercise because it shows how much better a group can reason than even the most knowledgeable individual. My Swiss counterpart wondered why I had bothered to suggest this, since most Swiss would take that conclusion for granted. In their view, it was only

Americans who needed to learn the lesson that group results can be better than even the best individual results.

To examine the implications (for organizations) of such national culture differences, it is helpful to use some of the dimensions used by anthropologists for comparing cultures.[1] These deeper dimensions are also reflected in the artifacts you observe in organizations, but they are sometimes not reflected in the espoused values. For example, a company espousing teamwork does not necessarily operate from a deep assumption that teams are better. In fact, the irony is that you often find that the espoused values reflect the areas in which the organization is particularly *ineffective* because it operates from contradictory tacit assumptions.

To get at the tacit assumptions at this level, you must see where the artifacts and values do not mesh and ask the deeper question of what is driving or determining the observed artifacts and daily behavior. For example, in the organization that espouses teamwork, if all of the incentive, reward, and control systems are based on individual accountability, then you can safely identify an operative tacit assumption that the individual really counts, not the team. In organizations that espouse employee empowerment and involvement, you sometimes discover that management assumes it has the right and obligation to issue commands as needed, to own all the financial information, to make all the decisions that affect the company, and to treat the employees as a replaceable resource. It is then no surprise to discover that the involvement programs are not working well in such an organization. Organizations that claim to be totally customer-oriented are sometimes found to develop marketing programs that border on lying and are willing to sell customers things that they don't need because of a deeper assumption that only the owner-shareholder interests should drive financial decisions, based on a deep assumption about the nature of capitalism. These deeper assumptions are often difficult to decipher, yet they are the real drivers of how the culture works at the operational level.

Assumptions About the Relationship of Humans to Nature

Cultures differ in whether they believe that humans should have a dominant, symbiotic, or passive relationship to the natural environment. Thus in proactive Western societies, we assume that humans can dominate nature, that anything is possible. The U.S. Marine Corps's slogan, "Can do," symbolizes this orientation and is reflected in a further slogan: "The impossible just takes a little longer." By contrast, in many Asian societies it is assumed that humans should blend into nature, or even make themselves submissive to nature. The natural environment is assumed to be more immutable, and the best way to be "human" is to blend with it.

In the organizational arena, these assumptions have their counterpart in that some organizations assume they will take a dominant market position and "define" the market, while others seek a niche and try to fit into it as best they can. Since business philosophy globally is to a large degree a reflection of modern Western society, the assumption has also grown up that it is advantageous to have a dominant position. There is research evidence supporting dominance assumptions, but this does not change the reality that in some other societies the so-called "correct" way to define a business is to find a niche and blend in.

Questions for the Reader

Ask yourself and others:

- How does your organization define itself relative to others in its industry, and what are its aspirations for the future?
- Does it view itself as dominating, just fitting into a niche, or passively accepting whatever the environment makes possible?

Assumptions About Human Nature

Cultures differ in the degree to which they assume that human nature is basically good or basically evil, and in the degree to which they assume that human nature is fixed or can be changed. In his classic book *The Human Side of Enterprise*, Douglas McGregor noted that U.S. managers differed greatly on this human nature dimension.[2] Some assumed that humans were basically lazy and would work only if given incentives and controls—what he called Theory X. Other managers assumed that humans were basically motivated to work and only needed to be given the appropriate resources and opportunities; this he called Theory Y. McGregor also argued that these tacit assumptions basically determined the managerial strategy that a given manager would use. If they did not trust employees, they would employ time clocks, monitor them frequently, and in other ways communicate their lack of trust. The eventual result would be that the employees would react by becoming more passive; of course, once this happened, the managers would feel that their original assumptions had been confirmed. Much of what we call today command-and-control systems have at their root this assumption that employees cannot be trusted.

On the other hand, managers who believed that employees could and would link their own goals to those of the organization would delegate more, function more as teachers and coaches, and help employees develop incentives and controls that they themselves would monitor. McGregor observed that Theory Y managers were more effective because they would bring out more motivation and creativity in employees, while, at the same time, having the flexibility to be autocratic and controlling if the task required it or they encountered employees who indeed could not be trusted. But again we must be cautious and note that not only may different cultural assumptions be appropriate to different kinds of tasks and circumstances, but also that overt managerial style may vary independent of whether the manager is Theory X or Theory Y. For example, there are numerous stories of American managers having trouble in French companies if they do not assert their authority forcefully at the outset. What an American employee might resent a French employee might expect.

A further important variation among cultures is the degree to which it is assumed that human nature is fixed or malleable. In most Western cultures, especially the United States, we endorse the view that we can be whatever we choose to be, as illustrated by the thousands of How to Improve Your . . . books that proliferate in airport bookstalls. In other cultures it is believed that human nature is fixed and that one must adapt as best one can to what one is.

Questions for the Reader

Ask yourself and others:

- What are the assumptions or "messages" behind the incentive, reward, and control systems in your organization? Do these systems communicate trust of employees, or mistrust?

- If you had to rate your organization on a 10-point scale (with 1 being totally Theory X, 10 totally Theory Y), how would your organization score? Would units of the organization reflect different assumptions?

- Do you believe that employees and managers can be developed, or do you basically have to select them for the right qualities? Which qualities are developable, and which ones are not?

Assumptions About Human Relationships

Is society basically organized around the group or community, or is society basically organized around the individual? If the individual's interests and those of the community (country) are in conflict, who is expected to make the sacrifice? In a groupist or communitarian society, as in Japan or China, it is clearly the individual who is expected to make the sacrifice. In an individualistic society like the United States, it is the group that must give in because individual rights are ultimately believed to be the basis of society. Thus in the United States it is possible for any citizen to sue even the U.S. government, a concept that does not even exist in the minds of citizens of a strongly communitarian society.

Organizations mirror this dimension in the extent to which they emphasize company loyalty and commitment versus individual freedom and autonomy. In strongly paternalistic companies such as C-G, it was expected that the company would take care of you and in return you would be loyal to the company and make sacrifices when necessary. On the other hand, at Apple and in many other Silicon Valley companies the assumption evolved that the company does not guarantee employment security and does not expect the employee to be loyal. Hewlett-Packard stands out in sharp contrast in having from the beginning espoused and practiced a more groupist paternalistic philosophy, symbolized most clearly by the 1970s incident in which everyone took a pay cut instead of laying people off. At the same time, in many of its work domains the individualistic assumption dominates, in that rewards, incentive, and controls are all based on individual performance.

If one looks at U.S. organizations in general, the clearest indicator of individualism is the sacred cow of individual accountability. No matter how much teamwork is touted in theory, it does not exist in practice until accountability itself is assigned to the whole team and until group pay and reward systems are instituted.

Questions for the Reader

Ask yourself and others:

- How much does your organization reflect deep individualistic versus groupist assumptions?

- How are incentives, rewards, and controls organized? If teamwork is espoused, how does it work out in practice?

- Does your organization expect you to be loyal? Do you expect the organization to be loyal to you and take care of you after a certain amount of time?

Assumptions About the Nature of Reality and Truth

In every culture, we grow up with beliefs and assumptions about when to take something to be *real* and *true*. In modern Western society, we begin with the belief that truth is what our parents, teachers, and other authority figures tell us, but then gradually we discover that the authorities often disagree on what is true, so we learn to trust our own experience and scientific proof. Finding things out for ourselves is rewarded and, in the end, we make science itself another sacred cow, as reflected in the advertising industry's obsession with statistics, scientific testing, and purported proof: "Research shows that this medicine will cure . . ." or "Doctors recommend . . .," with the implication that their authority also rests on science and research. Philosophically, we can think of this set of assumptions as ultimately pragmatic. We believe that which works.

But not all cultures are pragmatic in this sense. In many cultures, traditions, moral principles, religious doctrines, and other sources of ultimate authority define more clearly what is to be regarded as real and true. As we all know, even in Western society there are many arenas in which we take religious and moral authority to be more real than pragmatic experience. DEC reflected the ultimately pragmatic assumptions: everything had to be fought out, and only ideas that survived the debate could be true enough to be worthy of testing. The pragmatic test was further illustrated by DEC's willingness to support parallel competing projects and to "let the market decide." When DEC went into the personal computer market, it launched three different versions, but none of them survived. C-G, on the other hand, took it for granted that, since its evolution was based on chemistry and research, those with education and experience in this arena were qualified to define what was true. Whereas at DEC every idea was battled out—even if it came from founder Olsen or technical guru Gordon Bell—at C-G if a high-status senior researcher with a Ph.D. proposed an idea, then it was likely to be accepted.

Moral or religious principles come to dominate business decisions in some organizations, such as when, "on principle," a company refuses to go into debt or when personnel policies are governed by religious or moral principles. Thus in one organization lying is accepted as an inevitable consequence of politics, but in another organization the same behavior is severely punished on moral grounds. In a highly moralistic society, reality is often defined by the common moral code, whereas in a highly pragmatic society one ends up with some equivalent of the rule of law. In other words, the more pragmatic the society, the more common law and historical precedent come to be the court of last resort for conflict-resolution and for determining what is true, what really happened, or what should be done next.

In this cultural domain it is also useful to differentiate two classes of knowledge. Science and pragmatism work best in the realm of *physical reality*, defined by whether or not an assertion can be immediately tested. If I believe that this glass table will break if someone sits on it, that is testable. Science and pragmatism work less well in the realm of *social reality*, where immediate tests are not available. If I believe that glass tables are more attractive than wooden tables, this is not physically testable. It is in this realm that we rely more on consensus, on moral authority, and on conflict resolution mechanism such as the law. And it is in this realm that culture plays a bigger role in that a history of consensus on an issue makes group members feel that something is valid and true if it has worked in the past.

Between physical and social reality there are many gray areas in which we rely on a mixture of experience and moral or even physical authority. In most organizations their strategy, their means of implementing it, and even their measurement mechanisms are based on judgment and past experience rather than on scientific evidence. In the realm of economics and finance, there are broad principles that have research backing, but such principles rarely tell an organization whether a given strategy will, in fact, work or not. It is for this reason that we must recognize that culture heavily influences the fundamental mission and strategy by which an organization operates.

Questions for the Reader

Ask yourself and others:

- If you think of one or two key decisions that your organization has made in the last several years, what were the decisions ultimately based on? How was information defined? What was treated as a fact versus an opinion? What facts were decisive in making a decision, and what ultimately did the decision rest on? Was it facts, or opinions? If opinions, whose opinions mattered, and what gave those opinions credibility?

- If you had to rate your organization's decision-making style (with 1 being completely moralistic and 10 being completely pragmatic), where would you place it on the scale?

Assumptions About Time

Cultural assumptions about time and space are the hardest to decipher, yet the most decisive in determining how comfortable we feel in any given environment. If we look at assumptions about time first, cultures vary in the degree to which they view time as a linear resource, once spent never to be regained—what Edward Hall called "monochronic time."[3] With this concept, in any given unit of time only one thing can happen; hence we develop calendars and appointment books. Time is money and is to be spent carefully. We disapprove of "killing time."

Time can also be viewed as more cyclical and as a resource in which it is possible to do several things at once—what Hall called "polychronic time." When a doctor or dentist simultaneously processes several patients who are sitting in adjacent offices or when a senior person or parent "holds court" and is able to process the needs of several subordinates or children simultaneously, he or she is using polychronic time.[4]

Organizations differ in the meaning they attach to being on time or late. In Latin countries, being late might be regarded as fashionable and appropriate, while in northern European countries it is regarded as insulting. Arriving at work early and leaving late can have different symbolic meaning in different contexts; it could be taken as high commitment or as inability to be efficient. In the organizational context, an important dimension of time is whether it is viewed as controllable or not. Planning time as used by most managers assumes that one can speed things up or slow them down according to the needs of the moment. If something needs to be done soon, we "work around the clock" to meet the deadline. On the other hand, the R&D department is more likely to be working on "development time," especially in the field of biotech, implying that the development of certain processes cannot be speeded up.[5] The planner may want the baby in five months, but the developer says, "Sorry, it will take nine months." In some occupations, schedules and time planning are critical to meet windows of opportunity or to facilitate coordination. But in other occupations, such as biology or chemistry, time is measured more by how long things take.

Cultures and organizations differ in whether they live in the past, present, near future, or far future. Some organizations do their planning entirely in terms of their past history of success and failure, while others are highly tuned into the present opportunities and hazards, while still others think about the near or far future in deciding what to do next. Organizations also differ in what kinds of units of time are used for monitoring and assessment, or what Elliott Jaques called "discretionary time units"— the length of time an employee is left alone without being monitored.[6] Production workers might be monitored hourly or daily, supervisors daily or weekly, middle managers monthly, and senior managers and board members only annually.

Finally, time is the key to teamwork and coordination. When individual employees or organizational units are sequentially or simultaneously interdependent, the success of the outcome depends very much on the degree to which they "synchronize their watches" and work at the same pace. Cultures and tasks vary in the temporal latitude that is granted. For example, Swiss trains are notorious for leaving on time and only staying in the station a certain length of time, no matter how many people are still hurrying to get to the train.

In summary, the key point is that if people have different assumptions about how time works there is a high probability that they will offend each other, make each other anxious, and precipitate task failures where coordination was required.

Questions for the Reader

Ask yourself and others:

- What norms about time do you have in your organization?

(Continued)

- What does it mean to be late or early, or to come in early or leave early?

- Do meetings start on time? Do they end on time?

- When you make an appointment with someone, how much time do you feel is normal?

- Does it bother you to be doing two or more things at the same time?

- How does your organization react to missed targets or schedules?

Assumptions About Space

Space, like time, has important symbolic meanings. Open office layouts imply that people should be able to easily communicate with each other, while private offices and closed doors symbolize the need to think for oneself. In some cultures, "privacy" means being literally out of sight behind closed doors. In other cultures it is considered private if you are out of hearing range, even if you are visible.

The normal distance that people stand apart from each other symbolizes the formality of the relationship: the closer, the more the implication of intimacy. If someone with whom we do not feel intimate stands too close, we find ourselves being uncomfortable and backing up; if someone lets us move in more closely, we interpret it as willingness to become more intimate (as when we literally whisper secrets into someone's ear at very close range). Cultures differ in what is regarded as the normal distance for an ordinary conversation. When two people who have different assumptions about this distance try to converse, one will feel that his private space is being intruded into and will back up to normalize the distance, but the other person will move forward to normalize the distance from his or her point of view, leading to an uncomfortable ritual dance with neither party knowing exactly why he or she is uncomfortable. And worse, one will say that the other one is too aloof, while the other one will say that the first one is too pushy.

Assumptions about space reflect assumptions about individualism versus groupism. In Western individualistic society, we assume that the space in front of us is our own and we don't like it when someone steps in front of us or is in our lane when we are walking (or driving). This feeling is often expressed as discomfort when someone is "in our face" and is rigidly enforced when we get into lines. If we have to move, we ask someone to "hold our place" and, if possible, we minimize physical contact. In societies that are more groupist, members learn early in life that space is shared and one must accommodate to other people, objects, vehicles, and animals. Waiting lines break down into loose conglomerations in which everyone jockeys for position and the inevitable physical contact is ignored as being impersonal and normal.

Where we place offices and desks symbolizes status and rank. Usually the higher the rank, the higher up in the building the office is located and the more it is surrounded by physical barriers to ensure privacy. The location and size of offices as well as the furnishings are in many organizations directly correlated with rank. We joke about status symbols such as wall-to-wall carpeting or having a window overlooking a nice view, but these jokes reflect serious cultural assumptions about the meaning of physical things in the environment.

Questions for the Reader

Ask yourself and others:

- How does the physical layout in your organization reflect working style and status?

(Continued)

- How do people express their rank through physical and spatial behavior?
- How do you organize the space around you, and what are you trying to communicate with how you do it?
- How is privacy defined in terms of physical layout?

Dealing with the Unknowable and Uncontrollable

One of the most important elements of culture is the set of assumptions that evolve to provide comfort when dealing with the uncontrollable and the unpredictable. At the extremes, it is not surprising that most cultures develop religious beliefs and concepts of God and Gods around those elements in their environment that are powerful but out of their control—sun, wind, fire, water, and other natural forces. Nor is it surprising that in our own contemporary cultures religion deals with birth, death, and the afterlife.

On a more mundane level organizational culture elements evolve around things that are out of control in the daily work life. For example, in a study of the adoption of computerized tomography in several clinics, Steve Barley observed that operators developed what amounted to superstitious behavior whenever the computer went down.[7] The rule was to call the engineer, but while waiting for him or her, the operators would try all sorts of things—even kicking the machine. As was typical in this technology, the computer would sometimes come back on, leading the technician to write down exactly what had been done just before the computer restarted. When the engineer arrived, the tech was told in no uncertain terms that he or she should have left things alone and that, in any case, what he or she did could not possibly have had anything to do with the restarting. Nevertheless the little notebooks of what techs did would be solemnly passed to new techs with the instructions: "When the computer goes down, you might try this . . . ."

As I have watched decision making at high levels in organizations, especially in the realm of marketing and finance, it often seems that the final decision is based on little more than experience, faith, and hope.

Questions for the Reader

Think about the areas of your work or life that are least under your control and ask yourself how you "plan" for those areas.

* What do you do to avoid bad outcomes?

The Bottom Line

Why is it important to know all of these distinctions about cultural dimensions? What difference does it make in daily life? I have already argued that culture is deep, stable, and complex. I have now added in the last two chapters that culture is also extensive—we have learned tacit shared assumptions about all areas of our lives. Culture, therefore, influences how you think and feel as well as how you act, and it provides meaning and predictability in your daily life. But it operates out of awareness. Cultural assumptions are tacit and taken for granted.

The question then arises, why do you need to analyze and assess culture in the first place? This is an important question not to be taken lightly. Understanding your culture is not automatically valuable, just as understanding your personality is not automatically valuable. It only becomes valuable and necessary if such understanding enables you to solve a problem, to make a change, to learn something new. Then you need to know how your culture would aid or hinder you, and then you need to assess some of the many dimensions that have been reviewed above. If things don't go right, if your organization is not achieving goals, or if you think you can do better, then you do need to get in touch with the deeper cultural assumptions that are driving you.

In the next chapter we will examine: When and how do we assess culture? Can one determine culture with a well-designed questionnaire? And, if not, what practical alternatives are there?

5

WHEN AND HOW TO ASSESS YOUR CULTURE

Culture assessment comes into play when an organization identifies problems in how it operates or as a part of a strategic redirection relating to mergers, acquisitions, joint ventures, partnerships, or other projects and collaborations in which more than one culture will be involved. In the absence of a problem to be solved or some new strategic goal to be achieved, culture analysis turns out to be boring and often fruitless. The potential insights that culture can bring to you will occur only when you discover that some problem you are trying to solve or some change that you are trying to make depends very much on cultural forces operating within you and within your organization. One of the first of these insights will be that cultural assumptions are the source of your identity and your strength. The things that you may feel need to be changed may be describable as necessary "culture changes," but you will find that they involve only parts of the culture, and most of the culture will actually help you in making those changes.

By answering the Questions for the Reader in Chapters Three and Four, you have begun this self-assessment. But your ability to decipher your own culture is limited because so much of culture is tacit. What techniques other than self-reflection are available to you?

Should You Use a Survey?

Most managers are measurement-oriented. It is part of the culture of management. The tacit assumption in the pragmatic,

U.S. managerial culture is that quantification is a good thing and provides precision. So you probably want to know right away whether there are surveys available that allow you to measure your culture and put numbers on all of the dimensions reviewed in the preceding chapters. You will find that there are indeed many surveys that will *claim* to measure culture, so how will you decide whether or not to use any of them? For example, a currently popular survey claims to tell you where your company stands in terms of two key dimensions: (1) how flexible your organization is and (2) how internally or externally oriented your organization is, leading to four types of "cultures":[1]

- Clan: Flexible and internally oriented
- Hierarchy: Stable and internally oriented
- Adhocracy: Flexible and externally oriented
- Market: Stable and externally oriented

Another survey offers to measure your company on its degree of sociability and solidarity, also leading to four types of cultures:[2]

- Networked: High sociability and solidarity
- Communal: High sociability and low solidarity
- Mercenary: Low sociability and high solidarity
- Fragmented: Low on both

A multi-dimensional survey developed by a European consulting company provides a profile of the organization and tries to show what a profile of an effective organization would look like.[3] The main problem in using any of these surveys is that the dimensions they measure may not be relevant to the problems you are trying to solve. It may be interesting to know that your organization is communal or fragmented, but it may have nothing to with what you are trying to do. Apart from this general objection to surveys for cultural assessment, there are further practical reasons limiting their utility.

Why Culture Surveys Do Not and Cannot Measure Culture

- You don't know what to ask, what questions to put on the survey, because you don't know at the outset what issues or dimensions are the important ones in your corporate culture and subcultures in relation to the problem you are trying to solve.

- You will risk measuring only superficial characteristics of the culture because survey instruments cannot get at the deeper tacit assumptions.

- Individual respondents will misinterpret or misunderstand some questions and, therefore, will provide unreliable information.

- You will not be able to perceive the interaction and patterning in the culture and the subcultures.

- It is very inefficient to try to infer *shared* assumptions from individual responses because of individual differences in how questions are perceived.

- The survey or interview process raises questions for participants and builds expectations to which you may not be willing or able to respond.

For example, as has been pointed out, it is common for companies to espouse teamwork, and surveys often reveal that employees wish there were more teamwork, more trust among employees, and so on. However, examining the artifacts typically shows reward, incentive, and discipline systems that put a premium on individual accomplishment and competition among employees for the scarce promotional opportunities that are available. If the company really wanted to become team-based, it would have to replace those individualistic systems that have worked in the past and are deeply embedded in people's thinking. If the company cannot or will not create group incentives and group accountability, the end result could well be a drop in morale as employees discover that what they hoped for is not happening.

In other words, what is often labeled as the "desired culture" and is measured by employee surveys that ask "What do you have now?" and "What would you like to see in the future?" is nothing more than a set of espoused values that may simply not be tenable in the existing culture. We can espouse teamwork, openness of communication, empowered employees who make responsible decisions, high levels of trust, and consensus-based decision making in flat and lean organizations until we are blue in the face. But the harsh reality is that, in most corporate cultures, these practices don't exist because the cultures were built on deep assumptions of hierarchy, tight controls, managerial prerogatives, limited communication to employees, and the assumption that management and employees are basically in conflict anyway—a truth symbolized by the presence of unions, grievance procedures, the right to strike, and other artifacts that tell us what the tacit cultural assumptions really are. These assumptions are likely to be deeply embedded and do not change just because a new management group announces a "new culture." As we see in the later chapters, if such assumptions really are to change, we need a major organizational transformation effort.

Can You Infer Culture from Self-Analysis?

Another way to understand why it is hard to *measure* culture is to analyze the layers of culture in your own personality. In the process of growing up, you become a member of cultural units that leave their residue in your personality and mental outlook. The most obvious manifestation is the language or languages you speak, which clearly you learn (they are not genetic) and which determine to a great degree your thought process and how you perceive the world. Beyond language are the many attitudes and values you pick up in your family, school, and peer group. It has been shown over and over again that kids show patterns of attitudes and values that are systematically different according to the community and socioeconomic strata in which they grew up.

A useful exercise is to ask yourself now, as an adult, what groups and communities you belong to and identify yourself with. Pay special attention to your "occupational community."[4] If you are an engineer doing engineering work, chances are you have a whole set of assumptions about the nature of the world that you learned as part of your formal education and in your early job experiences. On the other hand, if you have always been interested in selling, took a business course in school, and are working your way along in a sales and marketing career, you probably hold assumptions reflecting that occupational community. Notice that, as a salesperson, you often disagree with engineers and may even become angry at their outlook, forgetting that you and they see the world through the differing lenses of your own cultural educations. Your political beliefs, your spirituality or religion, and your personal tastes and hobbies all reflect the kinds of groups you grew up in and belong to in the present.

We know this intuitively and realize that we are products of our environments. What a cultural perspective adds to this insight, however, is recognition that your *current* outlook, attitudes, and assumptions are also a reflection of *present* group and community memberships, and that one of the reasons you and others cling to your culture is that you do not want to be a deviant in the groups that you value. In other words, one reason why cultural assumptions are so stable and strong is that they are shared and that the need to remain in the group keeps them active. To look ahead, let me point out that when we advocate "changing" culture, we are, in effect, asking that entire groups and communities alter one of the shared characteristics that may be central to their identity. No wonder it is so difficult; no wonder people resist change so much.

Questions for the Reader

Think through what groups and communities you belong to. Rank them in terms of their importance to you in the present and in the future. For each group or community, list some key assumptions, attitudes, beliefs, and values it holds. Use the categories in Exhibit 3.1 as a guideline.

Allow yourself to be surprised by how much of your personality and character—your thought processes, perceptions, feelings, and attitudes—are shared with other members of the communities to which you belong. Although we operate in life as individual actors, we are far more embedded in groups than we realize.

In conclusion, personal reflection about your present group and organizational memberships is a good start toward cultural analysis, but it still leaves unclear how much is actually shared. Having argued that a survey will not answer this question for the various reasons given above, how then should you proceed to do a culture assessment? If you do need to understand better how the corporate culture and its various subcultures will aid or hinder you in solving your business/organizational problems, how then do you proceed?

Deciphering Your Company's Culture: A Four-Hour Exercise

Remember that cultural assumptions are shared, tacit, and out of awareness. This does not mean that they are repressed or unavailable. If you want to access your organization's culture, bring together a group of employees who represent the parts of the organization that may be most involved with solving the business problem that is motivating this exercise. Remember, the process only works when there is a real problem to be solved. Bring in a facilitator who knows a little about the concept of culture and who does not belong to the group that is doing the exercise. That can be an insider from another department, an outside expert, or even you—if you are dealing mostly with people from other groups. The insider who is driving the change initiative should then work with the facilitator to select one or more groups that will become the "culture decipherers." The group of ten to fifteen should be people who cut across the levels and functions that are most likely to care about the business problem you are trying to work on.

1. Meet in a comfortable room with lots of wall space to hang flip-chart paper. Sit in a circle to facilitate face-to-face communication.

2. *State the business problem* (30 minutes). Start the meeting with a review of your "business problem"—something you need to fix, something that could work better, or some new strategy that you need to launch. Focus on concrete areas of improvement, or else the culture analysis may seem pointless and stale. State what the *behavior* would be in the future if the change program is successful.

3. *Review the concept of culture and its levels* (15 minutes). Once you agree on the strategic or tactical goals—the things you want to change or improve—review the concept of culture as existing at the three levels of visible artifacts, espoused values, and shared tacit assumptions. Make sure that all the members of the working group understand that the purpose of this model is to help members get to the deeper levels of the culture—the shared tacit assumptions.

4. *Identify and list artifacts* (60 minutes). Start by identifying lots of the artifacts that characterize your organization. Ask the newest members of the organization what it is like to come to work there. What artifacts do they notice? Write down

on flip charts all the items that come up. Use Exhibit 5.1 as a thought starter to make sure you cover all of the areas in which cultural artifacts are visible. You will find that, as the group gets started, all the participants will chime in with things they notice. You will see from the reactions of others which things are common and strongly felt. You might fill five to ten pages of chart paper. Tape them up so that the culture's manifestations are symbolically surrounding you.

Exhibit 5.1. Some Categories for Identifying Artifacts

- Dress codes
- Level of formality in authority relationships
- Working hours
- Meetings (how often, how run, timing)
- How are decisions made?
- Communication: How do you learn stuff?
- Social events
- Jargon, uniforms, identity symbols
- Rites and rituals
- Disagreements and conflicts: How are they handled?
- Balance between work and family

---

5. *Identify your organization's espoused values* (30 minutes). After an hour or so, shift gears and ask the group to list some of the espoused values that the organization holds. Some of these may have already been mentioned, but list them on pages separate from the artifacts. Some of these may have been written down and published. Sometimes they have been reiterated as part of the "vision" of how the organization should be operating in the future to remain viable

and competitive. Many of these will be identified as "the culture."

6. *Compare values with artifacts* (60 minutes). As the values are listed in the previous step, begin to cross-check those values against the artifacts. Next, compare the espoused values with the artifacts in those same areas. For example, if "customer focus" is espoused as a value, see what systems of reward or accountability you have identified as artifacts and whether they support customer focus. If they do not, you have identified an area in which a deeper tacit assumption is operating and driving the systems. You now have to search for that deeper assumption and write it down on another sheet.

To use another example, you may espouse the value of "open communication" and "open-door policies" with respect to bosses, yet you may find that whistle-blowers and employees who bring bad news are punished. You may have detected, among your artifacts, that employees are not supposed to mention problems unless they have a solution in mind. These inconsistencies tell you that, at the level of shared tacit assumptions, your culture may really be closed, that only positive communications are valued, and that if you cannot come up with a solution to the problem you are bringing up, you should keep your mouth shut.

As a general principle, the way to deeper cultural levels is through identifying the inconsistencies and conflicts you observe between (1) overt behavior, policies, rules, and practices (the artifacts) and (2) the espoused values as formulated in vision statements, policies, and other managerial communications. You must then identify what is really driving the overt behavior and other artifacts. This is where the important elements of the culture are embedded. As you uncover deep shared assumptions, write them down on a separate page. You will begin to see what the patterns are among those assumptions, and which ones seem to really drive the system in the sense that they explain the presence of most of the artifacts that you have listed.

7. *Assess the shared assumptions* (45 minutes). It is now time to assess the pattern of shared basic assumptions you have identified in terms of how they will aid or hinder you in accomplishing the goals you set out in the first step of this process (defining the business problem). Since culture is very difficult to change, focus most of your energy on identifying the assumptions that can *help* you. Try to see your culture as a positive force to be used, rather than a constraint to be overcome. If you see specific assumptions that are real constraints, then you must make a plan to change those elements of the culture. These changes can best be made by taking advantage of the positive, supportive elements of your culture, as will be explained later.

8. *Decide next steps* (45 minutes). The steps outlined above will lead to one of several conclusions. You may now have sufficient insight to plan the next steps in your change program, using culture to aid you and identifying cultural elements that will require culture evolution. You may discover that this group's analysis does not clarify the culture sufficiently or that differences among the members reflect the presence of subcultures that would require separate assessment. Or you may decide that you want additional groups to cross-check what you have learned so far.

   a. Repeat the process with other groups. If the picture formed from this meeting is incomplete or muddy, repeat the process with one or more other groups. If you think there might be subgroups with their own shared assumptions, test your thought by bringing together groups that reflect those possible differences. If you need to repeat this process several times (using about three or four hours each time), you are still far ahead of the game in terms of time and energy invested relative to doing a major survey by either questionnaire or individual interviews. The data you obtain are also more meaningful and valid.

b. Proceed with the change program using cultural strengths. Because you and the others in the group are "in" the culture you will be able to perceive strengths that outsiders might not notice. You then go back to the planning of your change program for the business problem you identified and examine systematically how the culture can help you accomplish your goals. If you also perceive that some elements of the culture will be obstacles or hindrances, you proceed to go to step 8c and define the overcoming of these obstacles as a new change initiative that you then have to launch.

c. Proceed with a culture change program to overcome barriers. If some cultural elements clearly prevent you from achieving your business goals, you must design a culture change program, realizing, however, that you are only proposing to change some elements of the culture. One step then, which will be illustrated later, is to see how some of the cultural strengths can help you change those cultural elements that need to be changed.

Case Examples and Analyses

The following cases can be viewed from several perspectives, depending on whether you, the reader, are a manager doing the change, a facilitator who will be running the workshop, or a member of one of the assessment groups.

Case 5.1. AMOCO Engineering

This case illustrates the culture-deciphering process in a project that did not initially involve the total corporate culture directly but instead required that we clarify the corporate culture in relationship to the engineering subculture to accomplish the goals of the project. It also shows that the assessment process is not a one-shot deal but evolves as the change project itself evolves.

In the 1990s "AMOCO Oil" restructured its internal engineering operations by combining all of engineering into a single service group. Previously, the eight hundred engineers involved had been working for various business units, refineries, and exploration and production units as members of those organizations. In the new, centralized organization, they would work as consultants to those organizations and charge for their services. The formal rules were that all engineering services would be charged for, with the fees to the various internal customers sufficient to cover the costs of running the eight-hundred-person engineering unit. The business units that would "hire" engineers to build and maintain the exploration, production, refining, and marketing activities could either use the internal central group or go outside for those services. However, the engineering services unit could only sell its services internally.

I learned all of this from the internal OD manager assigned to this central services group, whom we will call Mary. She was charged by the manager of the unit with forming a "culture committee," whose mission was to define the so-called new culture of this unit as it evolved into its new role. Mary decided that she needed an outside resource to think through the culture issues and hired me as a consultant to the project. We recognized that the individual engineers faced a major change in role and identity, from being members of a business unit to being freelance consultants who now had to sell themselves and their services, and who had to bill for their time according to a pre-set rate.

Mary recognized that creating a new culture in this unit was intimately connected to the existing culture in the larger company, since both the engineers and their customers were long-time employees of AMOCO. We also recognized that the engineers were coming from different subcultures, so it might not be easy for them to learn together and become one organization. In addition, once the engineering group was together, their occupational subculture of engineering would influence how they felt about their new role.

After several hours of conversation with Mary to plan how the culture committee could function effectively and what kinds of intervention might be needed, we decided that we had to do an assessment of AMOCO's *corporate* culture in order to get a sense of what kinds of assumptions these engineers were bringing with them from their various corporate projects. Mary selected fifteen engineers as a representative cross-section of the new organization, and we announced a half-day (four-hour) workshop to explore the AMOCO culture and its relationship to this new organization. I helped design the workshop and facilitated it.

1. We first polled the group to gain consensus on the business problem: the evolution of a new way of working and new values for the service unit in the context of the realities of the AMOCO culture.

2. I explained the culture model and the three levels.

3. We asked the group to brainstorm artifacts.

4. As artifacts were revealed, we asked for the espoused values.

5. We then explored how the values and artifacts did or did not match and sought out the tacit assumptions when there was no match.

6. We then explored which of these assumptions would help or hinder the evolution of a new way of working in this unit.

The meeting was successful in identifying a number of important assumptions. Mary, some of her colleagues on the culture committee, and I all felt that one or more additional groups should be run to flesh out the picture and check our perceptions of what we were hearing. Over the next several months, two more groups were brought together for half-day meetings, leading to a coherent picture of the present corporate culture.

The motivation for articulating this picture was that the senior management committee of this new unit needed to be involved if new ways of working and values were to be promulgated. Giving them feedback on the culture as we were beginning to see it provided the agenda for a working session with this senior group. They would elaborate the culture assessment and then make some decisions on what action steps *they* needed to take to define a new way of working, consistent with their new values.

I decided to give the cultural feedback as much as possible in terms of the language that the assessment groups had used. I also decided at this stage to present the assumptions around the major cultural themes that came out in the group meetings. Exhibit 5.2 is the document that was shared with the management group at a two-hour meeting to discuss "the culture of AMOCO." The major categories of work, people/motivation, management, and climate were presented in PowerPoint, one at a time, with questions and comments from the group and from me. I also encouraged members of the group to comment on how accurate this was in their own experience. The document is long and detailed because we felt that group members had stated similar points in different ways and that it was important for management to see these various nuances.

Exhibit 5.2. Culture Themes Identified in the "AMOCO" Assessment Workshops

I. Assumptions about the nature of the work to be done:
- The organization is energized by identifying problems and developing fixes.
- It works by quick fixes of whatever problems are identified ("fire, ready, aim").

- It is assumed that if you break a problem down into small enough pieces and fix each piece, the big problem gets solved (blindness to interdependencies).

- Problems are recognized and named once variances get high enough. Management then steps in with a quick diagnosis and fix, sets up a new structure or remedial process, and then relaxes and does not follow through on implementation (for example, shortfall on cost recovery).

- We have a "hero" culture: waiting for problems to get serious, then fire-fighting and rewarding the successful fire fighters ("But remember, a culture that rewards fire-fighters breeds arsonists").

- Quick fixes are always new structures and processes, and once a new structure or process has been put in place, the job is done. Implementation is someone else's problem.

- All dilemmas and predicaments are viewed as problems to be solved and are thus subject to the quick structural-fix response.

- No sensitivity to the complexity of "soft" issues or the difficulties of implementation after a new structure or process is announced.

- Fixes are often the creation of teams or groups, and once a team is formed it is assumed that the job is done (but the culture is basically individualistic; hence, teams may not function well).

- Getting involved with implementation is avoided because it exposes you to failure.

- It is assumed that fixes will sell themselves.

II. Assumptions about people and their motivation:

- It is assumed that people can and will work on their own, that they are highly motivated and dedicated (that is, management does not have to micromanage).

(Continued)

- It is assumed that people will be successful; success is expected and taken for granted.

- It is assumed that people have no ego or social needs on the job.

- You must be willing to sacrifice for the company by working long hours, taking two briefcases home, etc. Nowadays, everyone has two jobs and is expected to be able to do them.

- It is assumed that groups can work on their own and set their own priorities (but there is a sense of lack of direction by management).

III. Assumptions about the management process:

- The organization is procedure- and numbers-driven.

- It is all about dollars and costs.

- Surfacing costs is a good thing.

- The organization is numbers-oriented (for example, numerical target for how many people to have in the organization).

- The organization operates with a command-and-control mentality.

- It is assumed that "management decides; others do" (example: when there are jobs to be filled, management just decides who will fill the jobs, with little or no consultation).

- There is very little accountability and great latitude, especially in the intangible or soft areas that are harder to measure.

- Teamwork is espoused, but the reward system (forced ranking) is highly individualistic, with emphasis on rewarding "heroes."

- Engineers run the company. You know who is an engineer right away; they are the golden boys who are white, male, tall, clean-cut, and aggressive but not combative.

- Company is an autocratic/paternalistic family that takes good care of its children (pays well and has generous—but not portable—retirement) provided they are loyal, hardworking, and successful. If they are somewhat anxious, that is normal and OK.
- A done deal is irreversible.

IV. The organizational "climate":

- Climate is egalitarian, friendly, low-key, and polite, but possibly vicious and blaming when backs are turned.
- We are a punitive, blaming culture.
- You never say you don't know or admit that you made a mistake.
- No one wants to admit to bad things, but people talk about bad things that happened to others.
- When mistakes or failures are identified, blame is assigned quickly and without much systemic analysis; the guilty are named, badmouthed, and labeled, which affects their future assignments, but no formal consequences follow.
- There are not many incentives to work together.
- A single mistake for which you are blamed can offset many successes and result in your being labeled and limited in future assignments and promotions.
- If you are labeled as having made a mistake, it affects whom you can work with in the future, so being negatively labeled can be very destructive to a career.
- Once you are labeled, it is forever; examples are "superior performer," "dinosaur," "not a team player," "high-potential," "low-potential," "not management material."
- Working overtime is the norm.
- Work is done through relationships, and you work with those people whom you know; you use the "old boy" network.

(Continued)

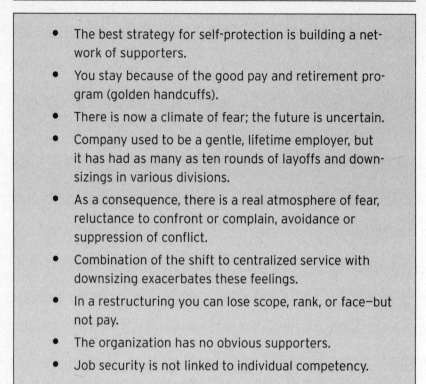

- The best strategy for self-protection is building a network of supporters.
- You stay because of the good pay and retirement program (golden handcuffs).
- There is now a climate of fear; the future is uncertain.
- Company used to be a gentle, lifetime employer, but it has had as many as ten rounds of layoffs and downsizings in various divisions.
- As a consequence, there is a real atmosphere of fear, reluctance to confront or complain, avoidance or suppression of conflict.
- Combination of the shift to centralized service with downsizing exacerbates these feelings.
- In a restructuring you can lose scope, rank, or face—but not pay.
- The organization has no obvious supporters.
- Job security is not linked to individual competency.

The management group basically bought this picture and confirmed with their own examples that the themes were accurately depicted. This reflection on their own culture allowed the senior management members to think through their own role. They recognized that the most difficult aspect of the AMOCO culture was the basic fear of being associated with any failure, or of being blamed for anything that went wrong. Furthermore, from the point of view of an engineering culture, they realized how hard it is for engineers to convert themselves into consultants selling themselves and charging clients by the hour.

These insights made it clear that the top priority for the project was to develop a new image of how to work that was consistent with the self-image they had. The culture committee was charged with coming up with a new set of values and practices—the "new way of working"—which would then be promulgated throughout the organization. Whereas in the past defining a "new culture" was thought of as a set of general values such as teamwork, this new way of working was to be a concrete description based on the culture assessment and the business realities that AMOCO faced. The new way of working had to deal with the structural realities of how the engineering job was now defined, but at the same time it had to fit the larger "blaming culture" in which the entire organization was embedded.

During the project, a live issue came up that illustrated the power of a cultural assumption like "You must never be associated with any failure because it can be career-threatening." A promising joint venture that was in the process of being created hit a major snag when it was discovered that the proposed project structure would put AMOCO engineers into situations in which they would be subordinate to project managers from the other member of the joint venture. The whole planning process unraveled because AMOCO engineers refused to work for someone from another company. They pointed out that, if a project failed, the manager from the other company could simply disappear, while their association with the failure would be negatively viewed within AMOCO. The fact that the *manager* was from the other company would not be viewed as a valid excuse within AMOCO.

To summarize, the impact of the cultural assessment was twofold. It made the senior leaders of the organization aware of the magnitude of the change task they faced, and it made them aware that just announcing a new set of values and goals would not produce the change they desired. Unless they could specify concretely what the new way of working was, they could not expect the engineers in the unit to adapt effectively to the new structural conditions imposed on them.

Mary and I continued to work on defining the new way of working by locating engineers who could be role models, who had made a successful transition to being "for-hire internal consultants." However, before this process went very far, British Petroleum acquired AMOCO and dismantled the central engineering group, launching yet another culture change of unknown dimensions!

Case 5.2. The "Delta" Sales Organization

This case illustrates how a culture assessment was necessary in order to make a critical succession decision. It also reflects the choices to be made in how the assessment is to be conducted.

Delta is the U.S. subsidiary of a large European pharmaceutical company. The vice president of sales had been in his job for thirty years and was widely credited with having built up a very successful sales organization. The culture issue came up around the question of whether to replace him after his retirement with an inside candidate, thereby reinforcing the sales subculture that had been built over a long time, or bringing in an outsider, thereby setting in motion cultural changes toward another type of sales organization. In this case, the goal of the assessment was not only to *understand* the present culture of the sales organization but also to *evaluate* it to see whether it should be perpetuated or changed.

I met with the top executive team and determined that they were indeed open to either alternative. What they wanted was an effective sales organization; they would measure this effectiveness by determining, first, how they felt about the culture that would be uncovered, and second, how the members of the sales organization felt about their own culture. The proposed assessment plan was for me to work my way down through the organization, doing individual or group interviews as seemed appropriate.

During the planning process with top management, an important issue came up. The current VP of sales expected me to do extensive individual interviews to decipher the culture. They had budgeted enough time and money to go through this lengthy process, based on their assumption that a picture of the culture would emerge from my processing all of this individual data. I had to convince him that it was not only more valid but far more efficient to work with groups, unless there was reason to believe that group members would be inhibited in talking about the culture in front of others. The result we agreed on was that I would interview individuals at the top level of the organization, where inhibition might operate; but as I got to the regional and district organizations I would run group meetings along the lines described above.

Exhibit 5.3 gives some excerpts from my report, which led eventually to the appointment of the inside candidate and reflected the decision to preserve and reinforce the existing culture. Notice that in this case the artifacts and values are more salient and the tacit assumptions are implied but were not made explicit. It is not necessary to have an explicit and complete picture of the whole culture and its tacit assumptions. The business problem may be solved without such an explicit analysis because the one or two tacit assumptions that are identified solve the problem.

The report illustrates how a culture assessment can be used to deal with a very specific question—in this case, a decision on senior management succession. If there had been more conflict or discord in the culture, the decision would have been more complex, but, as it turned out, throughout the organization

---

Exhibit 5.3. Excerpts from the "Delta" Sales Culture Report

- There is a very strong sales culture that was largely created over the last several decades by the present vice president, who is about to retire.

- This sales culture is credited with being the reason why the company has been as successful as it is.

- The present sales culture is perceived to be the company's best hope for the future. The sales organization feels strongly that it should not be tampered with.

(Continued)

- The key elements of the sales culture—its strengths—are:
  - The high morale, dedication, and loyalty of the sales reps
  - The high degree of flexibility of the reps in responding to changing management demands in marketing existing products
  - The high degree of openness of communication, which permits rapid problem solving, collaboration, and shifting of strategy when needed
  - Good communication and collaboration between district managers and reps
  - A strong family feeling, informal relationships up and down the hierarchy; everyone is known to management on a first-name basis and employees trust management
  - There is a strong development program that gives sales reps multiple career options according to their talents and needs
  - High ethical and professional standards in selling; focus on educating doctors, not just pushing individual products
  - High degree of discipline in following company directives in how to position products; feeling that "management showed us how to do it, and it worked"
- There was a strong feeling that only an insider would understand the culture they had built. Bringing in an outsider would be very risky because he or she might undermine or destroy the very things they felt made them effective.
- Although the culture is authoritarian and hierarchic, it works very well because top management gets across the message that it is the reps and the districts who make the system go and that what management is doing is in support of the front lines. It is a very people-oriented culture that allows for both flexibility and discipline. For example, every district follows the sales and marketing plan, but every district manager allows the reps to use their own skills and biases to their own best advantage and does not impose arbitrary methods to be used

in every case. Reps feel they have some autonomy, but feel obligated and committed to company plans.

- The individual and group incentive and bonus systems are working well in keeping an optimum balance between individual competition and teamwork. The management system is very sensitive to the need to balance these forces, and it does so at the higher level as well between the sales and marketing organizations.

- The wider company culture is very people-oriented and makes multiple career paths available. The emphasis on personal growth and development, supplemented by thorough training, emanates from the top of the company and is perceived as the reason why people are so motivated.

there was unanimity that the present culture was well adapted to the business situation and should therefore be preserved and enhanced. The inside candidate was therefore promoted with confidence that he would preserve and enhance the sales subculture that had been identified and described.

Case 5.3. Naval Research Labs

In this case the culture assessment was motivated by the presumption that the several subcultures of the lab would be in conflict with the subculture of the sponsoring organization. However, as will be seen, the actual assessment led to a completely unexpected set of insights about other subcultural dynamics that were actually operating. The initial goal was to identify and ameliorate the potential conflicts between local geographical subcultures of the Naval Research Lab located in New England and its administrative-political unit in Washington, D.C. The units had different populations and tasks, so it was anticipated that there would be important subcultural differences between the units and that those differences would create communication and allocation of resources problems with the different sponsors in Washington.

I was contacted by an MIT alumnus who worked in the labs and knew about my work on culture. He introduced me to senior management, and we decided to create a one-day assessment workshop in which we would explore the geographic subcultures, using my workshop methodology. The assessment was done with senior managers representing both the research and administrative units. We assumed that since the problems to be identified were top management issues, the assessment group should be primarily top managers from both the labs and the Washington sponsors.

As we proceeded to identify artifacts and espoused values, it was revealed that an important set of structural differences not previously noticed had to be taken into account. The local units of the Naval Research Labs worked in terms of *projects*, and each project had discrete financial sponsorship from a particular government agency or Navy unit. Therefore, every local project had created its own administrative staff working in Washington to develop budgets, keep sponsors informed, and generally manage all of the external political issues that might come up.

What was originally perceived to be two potentially conflicting geographic units, one in Washington and one in New England, turned out to be nine vertically organized project units, each of which had both a New England and a Washington subunit! Furthermore, because it was so critical for each project to work smoothly, the geographic factor was overcome in all nine projects through multiple meetings and constant communication. Each project thus developed a subculture based on the nature of its work and its people, and there were indeed subcultural differences among the projects. But the original notion that there was a geographic problem had to be dropped completely.

The important learning from this exercise was that the focus on culture revealed some structures in the organization that had not really been noticed or were thought to be significant. Where geographic separation mattered, each project team had already done a great deal to ameliorate the potential negative consequences.

The assessment revealed that the subcultures should be preserved rather than changed.

The Bottom Line

I have tried in this chapter to convince you of several things:

- Culture can be assessed by means of individual and group interview processes, with group interviews being by far the better method in terms of both validity and efficiency. Such assessments can be usefully made in as little as half a day.

- Culture cannot be assessed by means of surveys or questionnaires because one does not know what to ask, cannot judge the reliability and validity of the responses, and may not want to influence the organization in unknown ways through the survey itself.

- Survey responses can be viewed as cultural artifacts and as reflections of the organization's climate, but they are not a reliable indicator of the deeper shared tacit assumptions that are operating.

- A culture assessment is of little value unless it is tied to some organizational problem or issue. In other words, diagnosing a culture for its own sake is not only too vast a problem but also may be viewed as boring and useless. On the other hand, if the organization has a purpose, a new strategy, or a problem to be solved, then to determine how the culture impacts the issue is not only useful but in most cases necessary.

- Any issue should be related to the organization's effectiveness and stated as concretely as possible. "The culture" as a whole is rarely an issue or problem, but cultural elements can either aid or hinder the solution to the problem.

- The assessment process should first identify cultural assumptions and then assess them in terms of whether they are strengths or constraints on what the organization is trying to do. In most organizational change efforts, it is much easier to draw on the strengths of the culture than to overcome the constraints by changing the culture.

- In any cultural assessment process, one should be sensitive to the presence of subcultures and prepared to do separate assessments of them to determine their relevance to what the organization is trying to do.

- Culture can be described and assessed at the levels of artifacts, espoused values, and shared tacit assumptions. The importance of getting to the assumption level derives from the insight that, unless you understand the shared tacit assumptions, you cannot explain the discrepancies that almost always surface between espoused values and observed behavioral artifacts.

Now that you understand something of the process of cultural assessment, you are ready to think about how to build, evolve, enhance, or maybe even change culture.

Part Two

THE DYNAMICS OF CULTURE FORMATION, EVOLUTION, AND CHANGE

In order to understand the dynamics of culture, it is necessary to recognize that these dynamics vary hugely as a function of the growth stage of a group. In this part of the book, I will first provide a general model of learning and change, and then show how that model applies to culture formation in new organizations, culture evolution as those organizations grow, subculture dynamics as the organizations with different subcultures attempt to integrate, and, finally, change and destruction of cultural elements as organizations age and become dysfunctional.

6

CULTURAL LEARNING, UNLEARNING, AND TRANSFORMATIVE CHANGE

In order to understand the creation and evolution of culture and to manage culture change and transformation, you must understand learning and change theory in general. It is especially important to understand how learning and change work with human systems, in which the learners are adults who may have to *unlearn* something before they can learn something new. The fundamental reason why people sometimes "resist change" is that the new behavior to be learned requires some unlearning that they may be unwilling or unable to do. Adult learning is, therefore, fundamentally different from childhood learning, where everything learned is new. A model of learning and change that works for organizational employees must, therefore, take into account the fact of resistance to change and the reasons for it.

Resistance to change applies especially to cultural assumptions because, once cultural elements have stabilized in an organization, they provide meaning, predictability, and security to its members. If a culture change program is announced, discomfort and anxiety will be the immediate result because organization members will realize that they may have to give up some beliefs, attitudes, values, and assumptions—as well as to learn some new ones.

A Simplifying Model of Learning, Unlearning, and Transformative Change

One basic assumption of adult learning is that we are at all times in a state of what has been called a "quasi-stationary equilibrium" and that we are always trying to stabilize our emotional and cognitive state, which is perpetually bombarded by new external and internal stimuli that have the potential for upsetting and moving the equilibrium to a new state.[1] Many of these stimuli can be thought of as "driving forces" that push us toward something new, but we also generate within ourselves "restraining forces" that keep us at the present state. Learning or change takes place when the driving forces are greater than the restraining forces. This model is best understood from the perspective of a manager trying to produce change and can be viewed as consisting of several stages, shown in Exhibit 6.1.

This model of learning and change raises the controversial question: Is there a *natural* instinct to learn and improve? Is natural curiosity a motive to try new things and overcome old habits? Or must there be some sense of dissatisfaction for motivation to learn something new to arise? The organizational version of this question is, "Can a *successful* organization make

---

Exhibit 6.1 The Stages of Learning/Change

Stage 1. Unfreezing: Creating the motivation to change

   Disconfirmation

   Creation of survival anxiety or guilt

   Creation of psychological safety to overcome learning
   anxiety

Stage 2. Learning new concepts, new meanings for old concepts and new standards for judgment

   Imitation of and identification with role models

   Scanning for solutions and trial-and-error learning

Stage 3. Refreezing: Internalizing new concepts, meanings, and standards

   Incorporation into self-concept and identity

   Incorporation into ongoing relationships

major changes, or does there have to be some threat or sense of failure or crisis before people are motivated to make changes?" Must there be a "burning platform" or a major disaster or a public scandal before the need for real change is accepted?

Because humans avoid unpredictability and uncertainty, hence create cultures, the basic argument for adult learning is that indeed we do need some new stimulus to upset the equilibrium. The best way to think about such a stimulus is as "disconfirmation"; something is perceived or felt that is not expected and that upsets some of our beliefs or assumptions. Whether we feel it consciously or not, disconfirmation creates "survival anxiety"—that something bad will happen if we don't change—or "guilt"—we realize that we are not achieving our own ideals or goals.

Disconfirmation

Members of the organization can experience disconfirming forces directly, or they can be articulated by someone in the organization such as the CEO, a whistleblower, or a functional manager whose job it is to track certain indicators. Disconfirming information can involve any or all of the following categories:

- An economic threat—unless you change, you will go out of business, lose market share, or suffer some other loss
- A political threat—unless you change, some more powerful group will win out over you or gain some advantage
- A technological threat—unless you change, you will be obsolete
- A legal threat—unless you change, you will go to jail or pay heavy fines
- A moral threat—unless you change, you will be seen as selfish, evil, or socially irresponsible
- An internal discomfort—unless you change, you will not achieve some of your own goals and ideals

This last force, the internal one, is often thought of as the basis of "spontaneous" or natural learning, in that we seem to be able to motivate ourselves. We have a desire to do better, to achieve some ideal. But in my experience, such spontaneously motivated learning is almost always triggered by some new information that signals failure to achieve our own goals and ideals. I "spontaneously" decide to take some tennis lessons to improve my net game, but I realize that the reason for this decision is that someone whom I regularly beat is suddenly beating me.

Disaster and Scandal As Sources of Disconfirmation

For an organization, one of the most powerful triggers to change is the occurrence of a disaster and/or a scandal such as Three Mile Island, Challenger, Hurricane Katrina, the Texas City Refinery explosion, Enron, and, most recently the Wall Street-precipitated economic crisis. What such events reveal is that some of the ideals and values the organization espouses turn out not to be operational in practice. This leads to reassessment of what the deeper cultural assumptions are that are actually operating.

For example, in the recent economic crisis many financial institutions espoused the value of responsible lending in the housing market, yet their behavior showed blatant irresponsibility in making loans to consumers who could not possibly have kept up with the payments. The lenders rationalized their behavior by the assumption that housing values could only go up. Many of these organizations now recognize that their behavior was more motivated by the assumption that "we should maximize profits" than the assumption "we should only make loans to people who will be able to make payments no matter what." As more economic disconfirmation piles up, not only will companies reconsider their own assumptions, but the government will step in with more regulation.

In another example, a large multi-national company that prided itself on a career system that gave managers real choice in overseas assignments had to face reality when a key overseas executive killed himself and in his suicide note revealed that he had been pressured into the assignment despite personal and family objections. At the level of espoused values, the company had idealized its system. The scandal exposed the shared tacit assumption by which they really operated: that people were expected to go where senior executives wanted them to go. Recognizing the discrepancy then led to a whole program of revamping the career assignment system to bring espoused values and assumptions in line.

The Texas City disaster revealed that British Petroleum's announced policy of safety concerns was not supported by deeper assumptions. Cost cutting and ignoring warnings from the AMOCO people after the merger showed that economic assumptions were more operational than safety assumptions, leading Lord Brown, the CEO, to resign and new safety initiatives to be launched.

Introduction of New Technologies As a Source of Disconfirmation

New technology as a force for change is most visible in the impact that the introduction of computers and information technology has had on most organizations. Not only have employees had to learn how to operate the new hardware, but the networking and work-at-home options have disconfirmed many of the assumptions about how work could and should be done. Any new technology will force change in work behavior which will probably eventually impact cultural assumptions, but information technology has been especially significant as a force for change.

Mergers, Acquisitions, and Joint Ventures As Sources of Disconfirmation

When two or more cultures come together and try to work in concert many forces are unleashed that will disconfirm cultural elements in either or both organizations. Unfortunately, in most cases the need for culture assessment and possibly change arises only after the joint organization has been created, without consideration of whether the existing cultures were or were not compatible.

Charismatic Leadership As a Source of Disconfirmation

A new leader who is charismatic can sometimes create motivation to change by pointing out convincingly that "We are doing OK, but think how much better we could be doing if we learned how to do things in this new way." It takes charisma to get employees' attention, to avoid a complacent reaction that the bosses are only crying wolf. When a less-charismatic leader tries to convince the organization it is in trouble and must learn how to do some things differently in order to survive or grow, the message is often met with skepticism. Employees do not agree with the leaders' definition of trouble or they do not believe that the organization is in economic, political, technological, or legal trouble, especially if those leaders give themselves generous bonuses while touting cost-cutting. Employees often do not understand the economic situation well enough because they have never been educated in the economics of their business. They often do not trust management, believing instead that if they work harder or smarter they will ultimately be taken advantage of anyway. What makes charismatic leaders so powerful is their ability to overcome employee skepticism.

Education and Training As Sources of Disconfirmation

Many organizations have learned that the only way to convince employees and managers of the need to do things differently is by "educational interventions." As we just said, employees often do not believe what their leaders tell them unless they are educated to the economic realities of their business. A similar issue arises with respect to becoming responsible in the areas of environment, health, and safety. Employees do not accept the need for new, responsible behavior patterns until they have been educated about the dangers inherent in environmental events.

Change programs therefore often have to begin with educational efforts, which may take time and energy. Such programs do not disconfirm directly by challenging existing views but, rather, seduce the change targets by providing new and stimulating information that subtly challenges existing views. This kind of disconfirmation through seduction is especially relevant when there is enough time to educate employees and to lay the groundwork for more direct disconfirmation later.

Survival Anxiety (or Guilt) and Learning Anxiety

If the disconfirming data get through your denial and defensiveness, you will feel either *survival anxiety or guilt*. You do not necessarily feel anxiety or guilt directly, but you experience discomfort that something bad may happen to you if you don't respond in some way. You begin to recognize the need to change, the need to give up some old habits and ways of thinking, and the necessity of learning new habits and ways of thinking. But at the moment you accept the need to change, you also realize that the new behavior that may be required of you may be difficult to learn, and the new beliefs or values that are implied may be difficult to accept. This discomfort is best thought of as *learning anxiety*. The interaction of these two anxieties creates the complex dynamics of change.

The easiest way to illustrate this dynamic is in terms of learning a new stroke in tennis or golf. The process starts with disconfirmation: you are no longer winning against opponents you used to beat, or your aspirations for a better score or a better-looking game are not met. The felt need to do "something" is survival anxiety/guilt. You can, of course, exit from the situation and decide to give up tennis or accept playing at a lower level. When employees are confronted with required changes, they do have the choice of leaving the organization. But in most cases exit will either not be possible or not desirable, so you decide to improve your game.

But as you contemplate the actual process of unlearning your old stroke or swing and developing a new one, you realize that you may not be able to do it, or you may be temporarily incompetent during the learning process. These feelings are learning anxiety. Similar feelings arise in the cultural arena when the new learning involves becoming computer competent, changing supervisory style, transforming competitive relationships into teamwork and collaboration, replacing a high-quality, high-cost strategy with one that leads to being the low-cost producer, moving from engineering domination and product orientation to a marketing-and-customer orientation, learning to work in nonhierarchical, diffuse networks, and so on.

Psychological Basis of Learning Anxiety/ Resistance to Change

Learning anxiety is a combination of several specific fears, all of which may be active at any time as you contemplate having to unlearn something and learn something new.

Fear of Loss of Power or Position. The most common basis of resistance to change is the fear that with your new learning will come a new position that will be lower in the status hierarchy or less powerful than the position you now hold.

Fear of Temporary Incompetence. During the transition process, you do not feel competent because you have given up the old way and have not yet mastered the new one. The best examples probably are evident in efforts to learn to use a computer.

Fear of Punishment for Incompetence. If it takes you a long time to learn the new way of thinking and doing things, you will fear being punished for your lack of productivity. In the computer arena, there are striking cases in which employees never learn the new system sufficiently to take advantage of its potential because they feel they have to remain productive—so they spend insufficient time on the new learning.

Fear of Loss of Personal Identity. If your current way of thinking is a strong source of identity for you, you may not wish to be the kind of person the new culture requires you to be. For example, in the breakup of the Bell System, many old-time employees left because they could not accept the identity of being a member of a hard-driving, cost-conscious organization that would take phones away from consumers who could not afford them.

Fear of Loss of Group Membership. The shared assumptions that make up a culture also identify who is in and who is out of the group. In developing new ways of behaving and thinking, you become a deviant in your group and may be rejected, or even ostracized. To avoid losing group membership, you resist learning the new ways of thinking and behaving. This fourth force is perhaps the most difficult to overcome because it requires the whole group to change how it thinks, as well as its norms of inclusion and exclusion.

Defensive Responses to Learning Anxiety[2]

As long as your learning anxiety remains high, you are motivated to resist the validity of the disconfirming data or invent various excuses for why you cannot really engage in a transformative learning process right now. These responses come in definable stages.

Denial. You convince yourself that the disconfirming data are not valid, or are temporary, or don't really count, or reflect someone just crying "wolf," and so on.

Scapegoating, Passing the Buck, and Dodging. You convince yourself that the cause is in some other department, that the data do not apply to you, and that others need to change first before you do.

Maneuvering and Bargaining. You want special compensation for the effort to make the change; you want to be convinced that it is in your own interest and of long-range benefit to you; you will agree to change only if some others change as well.

Given these defensive responses and acknowledging their psychological validity, how then do you proceed to make change happen? How do you begin the learning process?

Two Principles of Learning and Change

If you are the change manager, how do you get past the resistance to change? Two principles come into play:

- *Principle One:* Survival anxiety or guilt must be greater than learning anxiety.
- *Principle Two:* Learning anxiety must be reduced rather than increasing survival anxiety.

The implementation of Principle Two means that the change process creates for you, the change target, a kind of "psychological safety"—that it is safe to abandon your old behavior and attempt to learn the new behavior.

From the change manager's point of view, it might seem obvious that the way to motivate you would be simply to increase the driving forces, heighten your survival anxiety, or make you feel even more guilty about failing to achieve your ideals. The problem with this approach is that, with greater threat or guilt, you may simply increase your defensiveness to avoid the threat or pain of the learning process. Or you may exit from the situation altogether. That realization leads to the key insight about learning and change embodied in Principle Two, that you can attempt to remove some of the restraining forces, that is, reduce the learning anxiety by increasing the learner's sense of "psychological safety." The learner needs reassurance that the pain of unlearning and relearning will be possible, worthwhile, and, most important, will be supported by the provision of whatever time and other resources are needed to facilitate the new learning.

How Do You Create Psychological Safety?

Creating psychological safety for organizational members who are undergoing change and learning involves a number of steps, and they must be taken almost simultaneously. I list them here chronologically, but the change manager must be prepared to implement all of them.

1. A *compelling positive vision*. If you are the target of change, you must believe that you and the organization will be better off if you learn the new way of thinking and working. The vision must be articulated (and widely held) by senior management. And, most important of all, the vision must articulate the desired "new way of working." If the learners do not understand the actual behavior that will be required of them, they cannot figure out what they will have to unlearn and how they will go about it. *The new way of working must be presented as necessary for the survival or growth of the organization and be perceived as non-negotiable.*

2. *Formal training*. If you are to learn new ways of thinking, new attitudes, and new skills, you must have access to whatever formal training is required. For example, if the new way of working necessitates teamwork, formal training on team building and maintenance must be provided.

3. *Involvement of the learner*. If the formal training is to take hold, you must have a sense that you can manage your own

informal method of learning. Everyone learns slightly differently, so it is essential to involve learners in designing their own optimal learning process. The goals of learning are nonnegotiable, *but the method of learning can be highly individual.*

4. *Informal training of relevant "family" groups and teams.* Because resistance to change is often embedded in group norms, informal training and practice must be provided to whole groups so that new norms and new assumptions can be built jointly. The learner should not feel deviant in deciding to engage in the new learning.

5. *Practice fields, coaches, and feedback.* You cannot learn something fundamentally new if you don't have the time, the resources, coaching, and valid feedback on how you are doing. Practice fields are particularly important so that you can make mistakes and learn from them without disrupting the organization.

6. *Positive role models.* The new way of thinking and behaving may be so different that you must see what it looks like before you can imagine yourself doing it. You must be able to see the new behavior and attitudes in others with whom you can identify.

7. *Support groups.* Groups should be formed in which problems connected with learning are aired and discussed. You must be able to talk about your frustrations and difficulties in learning with others who are experiencing similar difficulties so that you can support each other and jointly learn new ways of dealing with the difficulties.

8. *Systems and structures consistent with the desired changes.* It is essential to have reward and discipline systems and organizational structures consistent with the new way of thinking and working. For example, if you are learning how to be a team player, the reward system must be group-oriented, the discipline system must punish individually aggressive and selfish behavior, and the organizational structures

must make it possible to work as a team. Many change programs fail because the new way of working is not supported
by the organizational structures, rewards, or controls.

In summary, a change program that involves unlearning
and relearning requires that all eight of the above conditions be
met. If you consider the difficulty of achieving all eight, and the
energy and resources that have to be expended to accomplish
them, it is no small wonder that changes are often short-lived
or never get going at all. As one politician put it recently, "A
vision without funding is a hallucination." On the other hand,
as some of the cases in the next chapters will show, when an
organization sets out to truly transform itself, the eight conditions described can be created and significant cultural changes
can be achieved.

What Changes? Cognitive Redefinition

The best way to characterize the process of what actually happens in the learner is to call it "cognitive redefinition." On
the surface and in the short run, only overt behavior changes.
Employees can be coerced into the new way of working, and they
will continue to display the behavior as long as the surveillance
and threat of punishment are present. But no new learning has
taken place until the new behavior has been incorporated into
the learner's self-image—has been internalized. And that always
includes some new cognitions, some new definitions and standards of judgment. If you have been trained to think in a certain
way and are a member of a group that thinks the same way, you
have to begin to imagine changing to a new way of thinking.

If you were an engineer at AMOCO, you were a member of a division that used engineers as experts with technical resources, clear career lines, and a single boss. In the new
structure, you were now asked to think of yourself as a member
of a consulting organization that sells its services to customers
who can purchase them elsewhere if they do not like your deal.

To make such a transformation, you must develop several new concepts: "freelance consultant," "selling services for a fee," "competing with outsiders who can underbid you." In addition, you have to learn a new meaning for the concept of being an engineer and what it now means to be an employee of AMOCO. To achieve this you have to unlearn one of the central assumptions of the engineering culture that "engineering work speaks for itself, it does not have to be sold." You face a new reward system and are paid and promoted on your ability to bring in work. You must now see yourself as a salesman more than an engineer. Finally, you must define your career in quite different terms and learn to work for lots of bosses.

Along with new concepts come new standards of evaluation. Whereas in the former structure you were evaluated largely on the quality of your work and the engineering occupation operated on the assumption that you maximize quality and elegance no matter what the cost; you now have to estimate more accurately just how many days a given job will take, what quality level can be achieved in that time, and what it costs if you try for the higher-quality standard you are used to. The requirement to sell your service in a competitive market place forces you to evaluate your work against entirely different criteria than what you were used to.

The computer designers at DEC who tried to develop products competitive with the IBM PC never changed their standards of evaluation for what a customer expected. They over-designed the products, made them too expensive, and included far too many bells and whistles. The designers were embedded in their old way of thinking, and the organization did not have a change program powerful enough to help them cognitively redefine what the new marketplace needed.

In many change programs senior management announces a strategy of shifting from a production or engineering focus to a customer-centered marketing focus. When they do this they are asking many of their employees to make a major cognitive shift that they may not be able to make. When senior management announces they are going from a formal hierarchy to a matrix or networked project structure, they are asking their employees to grasp entirely alien concepts of how to work and how to think about authority. When senior management announces that employees should become more involved and empowered, they are asking both employees and supervisors to shift their whole cognitive frames of reference for what it means to be an employee or a supervisor.

Such cognitive shifts are possible if the organization manages to create enough psychological safety—especially if it involves the people who are the targets of change in the learning process. Then the learning takes place through either trial and error (based on the learner's scanning of the work environment to locate possible options for new behaviors) or a more formal training process (which usually involves imitating role models and psychologically identifying with them). For all of this to happen, the desired new behavior must be clearly defined and the learner must discover that the new behavior leads to desirable outcomes. Whereas initially the employee can be coerced into new behavior, only if that behavior leads to better outcomes will the employee begin to internalize new meanings and standards of judgment.

Imitation and Identification Versus Scanning and Trial and Error

There are two major mechanisms by which you learn new concepts, new meanings for old concepts, and new standards of evaluation. You learn through imitating a role model and psychologically identifying with that person, or you keep inventing your own solutions until something works for you.

If you are the change manager, you have a choice as to which mechanism to encourage. As part of a training program, you can provide role models through case materials, films, role plays, or simulations. You can bring in learners who have acquired the new concepts and encourage others to find out how they did it. This mechanism works best if it is clear what the new way of working is to be and if the concepts to be taught are themselves clear. However, we sometimes learn things through imitation only to find that they do not really fit into our personality or our ongoing relationships. Once we are on our own and the role models are no longer available, we revert to our old behavior.

Alternatively, if you want the learners to learn things that really fit into their personality, then you must withhold role models and encourage learners to scan their environment and develop their own solutions. For example, AMOCO could have developed a training program for how to be a consultant, built around engineers who had made the shift successfully. However, senior management felt that the shift was so personal that they decided merely to create the structure and the incentives, but let each engineer figure out for himself or herself how to manage the new kinds of relationships. In some cases, this meant that people left the organization. But those engineers who learned from their own experience how to be consultants genuinely evolved to a new kind of career, one that they integrated into their total lives.

The general principle here is that the change manager must be clear about the ultimate goals, the new way of working that is to be achieved. But this does not necessarily imply that everyone gets to the goal in the same way. Involving the learner does not imply that the learner has a choice about the ultimate goals, but it does imply personal choice of the means to get there.

Refreezing—Seeking a New Equilibrium

The final step in any transformative change process is to internalize the new concepts so that the new behavior now occurs automatically. If the behavior fits the rest of the learner's personality and is congruent with the expectations of important others in the learner's work and social environment, it becomes a stable part of the person, and eventually of the group. But note that if you learn some new concepts that lead to new behavior that does not fit into your work or social group, you will either revert to your old concepts and behavior if you value the group, or leave the group if you now value the new concepts and behavior more. Group disapproval or personal discomfort will act as new disconfirmation and launch a new learning process. As individuals we achieve some sense of stability by only incorporating those new elements that fit our personality and help us to maintain our important group memberships. As the world becomes more dynamic, groups will become more and more important as islands of stability.

The Bottom Line—Implications for Change Managers

If you are the change manager, you must think carefully about which outcomes you want. First, you must decide whether entire groups or units must adopt the new way. In most culture change programs, it is almost always the case that you want the entire work unit to adopt a new way of thinking and behaving, so the training should initially be geared to groups, not individuals.

As you examine the entire organization whose culture is to be changed, think in terms of the various workgroups, hierarchical levels, departments, geographical units, and so on. If only key individuals change, chances are that when they go back to their workgroups they will revert to the norms of those groups.

Second, you must decide whether or not the new way of thinking and behaving can be more or less standardized. If there is clear consensus on the new way, then you should provide role models and behavioral examples of the new way of thinking and behaving. This process speeds up the learning but also leads to adopting new behaviors that may not fit the learners, that fail to be internalized, and that are eventually abandoned. On the other hand, you can state clear behavioral goals but invite learners to develop their own solutions. This trial and error is a slower process, but it guarantees that whatever is learned is internalized. In this instance, you should withhold role models or clear examples.

Third, you must ensure that there is sufficient survival anxiety to induce some motivation to change, but then must work to reduce the learning anxiety by providing psychological safety.

How this all works out will be illustrated in the next few chapters in relation to the growth stage of the organization. If you are in a young and growing company, go to the next chapter; if you are in a mature company well past its founding stages, you may wish to skip to Chapter Eight or Nine.

Questions for the Reader

- Think back to a recent change that you made. Can you identify the disconfirming forces that motivated you to want to change?
- Once you were motivated to change, how did you go about it?
- What actually changed, and how did you ensure that the change would last?
- Now think back to a recent change that was required of you by your organization and answer the same questions.
- What was different between when you initiated the change and when you were required to make the change?

7

CULTURE CREATION, EVOLUTION, AND CHANGE IN START-UP COMPANIES

The nature of culture change depends upon what stage of growth an organization is in. In this and the next two chapters, I will describe the change processes and show you what is involved if you want to manage them during founding and growth; in a midlife and mature or declining organization; and in mergers, acquisitions, and various kinds of joint multicultural ventures.

Founding and Early Growth

The most salient cultural characteristic of young organizations is that they are the creation of founders and founding families. The personal beliefs, assumptions, and values of the entrepreneur or founder are imposed on the people he or she hires, and—if the organization is successful—they come to be shared, seen as correct, and eventually taken for granted. The shared beliefs, assumptions, and values then function in the organization as the basic glue that holds it together, the major source of the organization's sense of identity, and the major way of defining its distinctive competence.

At this stage, culture is the organization's primary asset, but it is repeatedly tested by being acted out. If it is reinforced, if the organization succeeds, the culture grows stronger. If the organization fails, the founders are likely to be thrown out and their assumptions will come to be challenged and probably abandoned. During the growth phase, if the basic criteria of success are met, the organization will be very resistant to disconfirming forces and will tend to deny their validity or rationalize that they are irrelevant, as will be seen in some of the examples, especially DEC.

The need for a lot of unlearning in a young organization is limited by the success of the founder in selecting employees who already have the beliefs, values, and assumptions that the founder holds. If the founder is clear, only congruent employees are hired. If the founder is not clear at the selection point, some employees will find themselves in cultural conflict with the organization and either will become socialized and acculturated, or will leave the organization. In other words, the young company does not need to be unfrozen because the founders can pre-select their employees or individually socialize them. How this socialization process works is illustrated in the following examples.

Case Example: "Jones Food"

Founder Harold Jones was an immigrant whose parents had started a corner grocery store in a large urban area in the 1930s. His parents, particularly his mother, taught him some basic attitudes toward customers and helped him form the vision that he could succeed in building a successful enterprise. He assumed from the beginning that if he did things right he would succeed and build a major organization that would bring him and his family a fortune. Ultimately, he built a large chain of supermarkets, department stores, and related businesses that dominated its market area for many decades.

Jones was the major ideological force in his company throughout its history and continued to impose his assumptions on the company until his death in his late seventies. He assumed that his primary mission was to supply a high-quality, reliable product to customers in clean, attractive surroundings. His customers' needs were the primary consideration in all major decisions. There are many stories about how Jones, as a young man operating the corner grocery store with his wife, gave customers credit and thus displayed trust in them. He always took products back if there was the slightest complaint, and he kept his store absolutely spotless to inspire customer confidence in his products. Each of these mandates later became a major policy in his chain of stores and was taught and reinforced by close personal supervision.

Jones believed that only personal example and close supervision would ensure subordinates' adequate performance. He would show up at his stores unexpectedly, inspect even minor details, and then-by personal example, by stories of how other stores were solving the problems identified, by articulating rules, and by exhortation-"teach" the staff what they should be doing. He often lost his temper and berated subordinates who did not follow the rules or principles that he laid down.

Jones expected his store managers to be highly visible, be very much on top of their own jobs, and supervise closely in the same way he did, reflecting deep assumptions about the nature of good management. These assumptions became a major theme in later years in his concept of "visible management," the assumption that a "good" manager always had to be around to set an example and teach subordinates the right way to do things.

The founding group in this company consisted essentially of Harold's three brothers. But one "lieutenant" who was not a family member was recruited early; along with the founder, he became the main culture creator and carrier. Sharing Jones's basic assumptions about how to run a business, he set up formal systems to ensure that those assumptions became the basis for operating realities. After Jones's death, this lieutenant continued to articulate the theory of visible management and tried to set a personal example of how to do it by continuing the same close supervisory policies that Jones had used.

One of Jones's assumptions was that one could win in the marketplace only by being highly innovative and technically on the forefront. He always encouraged his managers to try new approaches, brought in a variety of consultants who advocated new approaches to human resource management, started selection and development programs through assessment centers long before other companies tried this approach, and traveled to conventions and other businesses where new technological innovations were displayed, resulting in his company being one of the first to introduce barcode technology. He was always willing to experiment to improve the business. Jones's view of truth and reality was that one had to find it wherever one could, and therefore it was important to be open to the environment and never take it for granted that one had all the answers.

If things worked, Jones encouraged their adoption; if they did not, he ordered them dropped. Measuring results and solving problems were for him intensely personal matters, deriving from his theory of visible management. In addition to using a variety of traditional business measures, he always made it a point to visit all his stores personally; if he saw things not to his liking, he corrected them immediately and decisively, even if it meant someone had to go around the authority chain. He trusted only those managers who operated by assumptions similar to his own, and he clearly had favorites to whom he delegated more authority.

Power and authority in this organization remained very centralized, in that everyone knew Jones or his chief lieutenant could-and would-override decisions made by division or unit managers without consultation, and often peremptorily. The ultimate source of power—the voting shares of stock—were owned entirely by Jones and his wife, so that after his death his wife was in total control of the company.

Jones was interested in developing good managers throughout the organization, but he never assumed that sharing ownership through granting stock options would contribute to that process. He paid his key managers very well but did not share ownership, even with those who had been with the company throughout its history. In this area, the assumption was that ownership was strictly a family matter, to the point that he was not even willing to share stock with the man who was his chief lieutenant, close friend, and virtual co builder of the company.

Jones placed several family members in key managerial positions and gave them favored treatment in the form of good developmental jobs that would test them early for ultimate management potential. As the firm diversified, family members were made division heads, even though they often had relatively little management experience. If a family member performed poorly, he would be bolstered by having a good manager introduced under him; if the operation then improved, the relative would likely be given the credit. If things continued badly, the family member would be moved out, although with various face-saving excuses.

My introduction to the company concerned this dynamic. Jones had only daughters and had moved the husband of his oldest daughter into the presidency of his company. This man was a very congenial person but not trained for his general management position, so Jones authorized the creation of a management development program for the top twenty-five people in the organization (the hidden agenda was to teach his son-in-law something about management). Jones's chief lieutenant brought me in as a consultant and trainer in the program; I was told from the outset that part of the goal was to educate the son-in-law.

Peer relationships among non-family members inevitably became highly politicized. They were officially defined as "competitive," reflecting Jones's belief that interpersonal competition was desirable. Winners would be rewarded and losers discarded. However, since family members were in positions of power, one had to know how to stay on the good side of those family members without losing the trust of peers, on whom one was dependent.

Jones wanted open communication and a high level of trust among all members of the organization, but his own assumptions about the role of the family and the correct way to manage were, to a large degree, in conflict with each other. Many members of the organization banded together in a kind of mutual protection society, which developed a culture of its own. They were more loyal to each other than to the company and had a high rate of interaction, which bred assumptions and norms that became to some degree countercultural to the founder's.

Several things should be noted at this point. By definition, something becomes part of the culture only if it works, in the sense of making the organization successful and reducing the anxiety of the members (including Jones). His assumptions about how things should be done were congruent with the kind of environment in which he operated, so he and the founding group received strong reinforcement for those assumptions. As the company grew and prospered, Jones perceived more and more confirmation of his assumptions and thus felt confident that they were correct. Throughout his lifetime, he steadfastly adhered to those assumptions and did everything in his power to get others to accept them. However, as has been noted, some of the assumptions made non-family managers more anxious, thus leading to the formation of a counterculture.

Jones also learned that he had to share some concepts and assumptions with a great many other people. As the company grew and learned from its own experience, his assumptions gradually had to be modified in some areas. If not, he had to withdraw from active management of those areas. For example, in its diversification efforts, the company bought several production units that would enable it to integrate vertically in certain food and clothing lines where it was economically advantageous to do so. But when Jones learned that he knew relatively little about production, he brought in strong managers and gave them a great deal of autonomy. Some of the production divisions never acquired the culture of the main organization, and the heads of those divisions never enjoyed the status and security that insiders had.

Eventually, the founder also learned somewhat painfully that he did not send the clear and consistent signals he thought he did. Unable to perceive his own conflicts and inconsistencies, he could not understand why some of his best young managers failed to respond to his competitive incentives and even left the company. He thought he was adequately motivating them and could not see that for some of them the political climate, absence of stock options, and arbitrary rewarding of family members made their own career progress too uncertain. Jones was perplexed and angry about much of this, blaming the young managers while clinging to his assumptions and conflicts.

Following his death, the company experienced a long period of cultural turmoil because of the vacuum created by Jones's absence and the retirement of several other key culture carriers. But the basic philosophies of how to run stores were thoroughly embedded and remained. Various family members continued to run the company, although none of them possessed the business skills that Jones had.

With the retirement of the chief lieutenant, a period of instability set in, marked by the discovery that some of the managers who had been cultivated under Jones were not as strong and capable as had been assumed. None of his children or their spouses was able to take over the business decisively, so an outsider was brought in to run the company. This person predictably failed because he could not adapt to the culture and to the family.

After two more failures with CEOs drawn from other companies, the family turned to a manager who had originally been with Jones Food and subsequently made a fortune elsewhere in real estate enterprises. This manager stabilized the business because he had more credibility by virtue of his prior history and his knowledge of how to handle family members. Under his leadership, some of the original assumptions began to evolve in new directions. Eventually, the family decided to sell the Jones Company, and this manager and one of the cousins started a business of their own, which ended up competing with Jones Food.

One clear lesson from the Jones Food case is that a culture does not survive if the main culture carriers depart and if most members of the organization are to some degree conflicted because of the mixed messages from the leaders during the growth period. Jones Food had a strong culture, but the founder's own conflicts became embedded in that culture, creating conflict and—ultimately—lack of stability. What should also be noted is that, as a company grows and matures, subcultures and countercultures are inevitable, requiring more standardization, control through systems, and the evolution of new cultural elements dealing with business processes. More will be said about this in the next chapter.

The founding and culture growth process described in the Jones Company is common to most start-ups, even though the technology, market, and personality of the founder may be very different. The DEC story has many similarities with the Jones story. If one reviews the history of IBM, one can also see how strong founder values—in Thomas Watson Sr.'s obsession with sales and marketing—became embedded in IBM's culture. It was only during Watson Jr.'s tenure that the need for much more technology became evident. But the marketing culture remained and was reinforced by bringing in Gerstner, an outsider, when IBM's fortunes were waning. It is important, however, to note that he was a marketing expert and helped IBM to get back on track as a marketing company.[1]

How Founders and Leaders Embed Cultural Elements

How founders and leaders impose their assumptions and values can be summarized by looking at the various mechanisms described in Exhibit 7.1. By far, the most important of these mechanisms is the leader's own behavior. When it comes to culture creation and embedding, "walking the talk" has special significance in that new members pay far more attention to the walk

Exhibit 7.1. How Founders and Leaders Impose Their Values and Assumptions

I.   Primary embedding mechanisms

- What leaders pay attention to, measure, and control regularly
- How leaders react to critical incidents and organizational crises
- Observed criteria by which leaders allocate scarce resources
- Deliberate role modeling, teaching, and coaching
- Observed criteria by which leaders allocate rewards and status
- Observed criteria by which leaders recruit, select, promote, retire, and excommunicate organizational members

II. Secondary articulation and reinforcement mechanisms

- Organization design and structure
- Organizational systems and procedures
- Organizational rites and rituals
- Design of physical space, façades, and buildings
- Stories, legends, and myths about people and events
- Formal statements of organizational philosophy, values, and creed

than the talk. Especially important is what the leader attends to, measures, gets upset about, rewards, and punishes. The supporting mechanisms of structures and processes become more important in the organization's mid-life, as new generations of leaders are heavily influenced by these structures and processes. In extreme cases, these elements even determine what kind of person is accepted as the leader. But in a young and growing organization, the personal behavior of the leader is by far the most important determinant of how the culture is shaped.

Culture Learning, Evolution, and Change Mechanisms

The members of a young, successful company cling to their assumptions for two reasons. First, the assumptions are their own or they would not have joined the organization, and their own experience confirms them. Second, they continue to reflect the assumptions of the founder(s) or founding family, who still have the power that comes from ownership. If the founders say, "This is the way we will do it, and this is what I believe," then members jeopardize their careers if they say there is a better way that ought to be tried. If the organization is succeeding, they feel disrespectful to be challenging the beliefs of the "father figures." In other words, this kind of evolving culture is very strongly held.

The emphasis in this early stage is on differentiating oneself from the environment and from other organizations. To this end, the new organization makes its culture explicit, integrates it as much as possible, and teaches it firmly to newcomers (or selects them for reasons of initial compatibility). One also sees in young companies a bias toward certain business functions, which influences the kind of culture that arises. In Jones Food, there was a distinct bias toward retailing and customers, whereas in DEC the bias was clearly toward engineering and manufacturing. Not only was it difficult for DEC's other functions to acquire status and prestige, but professionals such as marketers were often told by managers who had been with the company from its origin that "marketers never know what they are talking about" and "marketing is not good because it lies to the customer instead of solving his or her problems." In Ciba-Geigy, the early bias toward science and research remained, even though the company was much older. Since R&D was historically the basis of the company's success, science was defined as the distinctive competence, even though more and more managers admitted overtly that the future hinged on marketing, tight financial controls, and efficient operations.

In summary, young cultures are strong because:

- The primary culture creators are still present.
- The culture helps the organization define itself and make its way into a potentially hostile environment.
- Many elements of the culture have been learned as defenses against anxiety as the organization struggles to build and maintain itself.

Proposals to deliberately change the culture, whether from inside or outside, are therefore likely to be totally ignored or resisted. Instead, dominant members or coalitions attempt to preserve and enhance the culture. The only force that might unfreeze such a situation is an external crisis of survival, in the form of a sharp drop in growth rate, loss of sales or profit, a major product failure, or some other event that cannot be ignored.[2] If such a crisis occurs, a transition to the next stage (being managed by an outsider) may automatically be launched. The crisis may discredit the founder and bring a new senior manager into the picture. If the founding organization itself stays intact, so does the culture.

How, then, does culture evolve in a successful growing organization? Which change processes can be actively managed, from the perspective of either a leader or a consultant? Several change processes can be identified:

1. Natural Evolution: General and Specific Adaptation

If the organization continues to be successful and if the founder or founding family is around for a long time, the culture evolves in small increments by continuing to assimilate what works best over the years. *General* evolution involves diversification, growing complexity, higher levels of differentiation and integration, and creative synthesis into new and higher forms. *Specific* evolution involves adapting specific parts of the organization to their particular environments, thus creating subcultures that eventually have an impact on the core culture. These mechanisms cause organizations within varied industries to develop distinct industry cultures. Thus, a high-technology company develops highly refined R&D skills, while a consumer products company in foods or cosmetics develops highly refined marketing skills. But in all of these cases I think of it as "natural" evolution because it is necessary adaptation to the realities that the organization encounters.

Such differences in adaptation reflect important underlying assumptions about the nature of the world and the actual growth experience of the organization. In addition, since the parts of the organization exist in different environments, each part evolves to adapt to its particular environment. As subgroups differentiate and subcultures develop, opportunities for major culture change arise, but in this stage differences are only tolerated and efforts are made to minimize them. These evolutionary processes happen whether you do anything specific or not, but if you become aware of the processes you can aid them by imparting insight that permits planning and guiding the evolutionary process.

In this kind of growth, one would see many mini examples of disconfirmation, defining the new behavior and enforcing it through the embedding mechanisms described. But the overall emphasis is on maintaining the culture rather than changing it.

2. Guided Evolution Through Insight and Planning

If you think of culture as a mechanism for making the world meaningful and predictable, for avoiding the anxiety that comes with unpredictability and meaninglessness, you can help members of the organization by making explicit the major cultural themes and elements. If you gain insight into what your shared assumptions are and why you hold on to them, there is a better chance of evaluating them to determine how functional they continue to be as the environment around you changes. The internal deciphering process described in Chapter Five typically has the effect of producing a level of cultural insight that allows a group to decide the direction of its future evolution. The key roles of the leader in this process are to recognize the need for such an intervention and to manage the internal assessment process. The leader in these situations becomes a counselor, coach, or process consultant to guide the organization's evolution. Cultural evolution can then be integrated into the overall planning process.

An example of change through this kind of insight occurred in "Gamma Tech," an engineering driven company that had always lived by the assumption that marketing was a useless function relative to others. It thrived on its engineering culture yet its survival increasingly depended on effective marketing. In assessing their own culture, senior managers discovered that they shared a very limited and negative definition of marketing, as "just merchandising the products we already have." With the help of an outside consultant, managers gained the insight that their definition of marketing was biased and limited. They were then able through educating themselves to redefine in their own minds that marketing included building up Gamma Tech's company image, improving the connection between customers and the product development functions, training the field sales force on the characteristics of the new products, developing a long-range product strategy, and integrating various product lines according to projections of where future customer needs would be.

Gamma Tech's managers suddenly realized that all of the specific things they needed to do better were, in fact, "marketing." They began to see in their marketing managers skills they had not observed before, and this permitted them to begin valuing their marketing peers and moving them into more central roles in the management process. From an assumption that marketing was useless, they moved to a belief that marketing might be highly valuable, by redefining in their minds what marketing was. As they paid attention to various marketing functions, success came-and they gradually adopted the assumption that marketing was crucial to their continued existence.

Many of the interventions that have occurred over the years in DEC can be seen as efforts to give the company insight into its own culture. For example, at one annual corporate seminar the company's poor performance was being discussed with the top eighty managers. A depressive mood overtook them and was finally articulated: "We could do better, if only our president or one of his key lieutenants would decide on a direction and tell us which way to go."

Those of us familiar with the culture heard this not as a realistic request but as a wish for a magic solution. I was scheduled to give a short presentation on the company's culture and used the opportunity to raise a question: "Given the history of this company and the kinds of managers and people you are, if Ken Olsen marched in here right now and told everyone in what directions he wanted you to go, do you think you would follow?" There was a long silence and then gradually a few knowing smiles. A more realistic discussion ensued. The group collectively realized that, given their history, they would not accept orders from above anyway—even from Olsen—and that they had better get busy to work out for themselves a new sense of direction. In effect, the group reaffirmed and strengthened its assumptions about individual responsibility and autonomy, but these senior managers also recognized that their wish for marching orders was really a wish for more discipline in the organization—and that this discipline could be achieved among themselves by tighter coordination at their own level. That they could not, in the end, achieve this coordination could also be inferred from other elements of the DEC culture—the empowerment of individuals and the assumption that internal competition is a good thing.

3. Managed Evolution Through Promotion of "Hybrids"

Changes in the environment often create disequilibria that force real cultural change. How can a young organization so highly committed to its identity make such changes? Clearly, the first condition is that key leaders in the organization notice the disconfirming information. In the young DEC there was a fairly systematic *disregard* of changes in the technology and market. Changes were noticed, but not taken seriously because the new behavior that DEC would have had to learn was so alien to their preferred innovative behavior that they chose to disregard much of the disconfirming information. On the other hand Jones food realized that, if they were to expand into production, they would need a different kind of business process. How to accomplish such a change?

One mechanism is to stimulate cultural evolution by systematically promoting hybrids who grew up in the culture and therefore understood it, but who developed some new beliefs and assumptions that were more congruent with the new behavior that would be required to remain adaptive. Because of their personalities or life experiences, or the subculture in which their careers developed, hybrids are employees or managers who hold assumptions that are in varying degrees different from those at the core and thus can move the organization gradually into new ways of thinking and acting. If such managers are put into key positions, they often elicit a feeling from others on the order of "We don't like what he or she is doing in the way of changing the place, but at least he or she is one of us." So not only does the hybrid get more initial acceptance, but he or she is familiar enough with the core culture to know how to use it as a positive force to make changes at the periphery.

For this mechanism to work, some of the company's most senior leaders must pay attention to disconfirming signals and have insight into what is missing. This implies that they must first become marginal enough in their own organization to be able to perceive their corporate culture accurately. They may obtain such insight through the questions of board members, from consultants, or through educational programs where they meet other leaders. If the leaders then recognize the need for change, they can begin to select for key jobs those members of the existing culture who best represent the new assumptions they want to enhance.

For example, at one stage in its history DEC found itself rapidly losing the ability to coordinate the efforts of large numbers of units. Olsen and other senior managers knew that bringing an outsider into a key position would be rejected, so they attempted to gradually fill several key positions with managers who had grown up in manufacturing and in field service, where discipline and centralization had been the norm. These managers operated within the culture but gradually tried to impose more centralization and discipline. Similarly, once Ciba-Geigy recognized the need to become more marketing-oriented, it began to appoint to senior positions managers who had grown up in the pharmaceutical division, where the importance of marketing had been recognized earlier. Organizations sometimes attempt to achieve such changes by bringing in outsiders, but at this stage the culture is too strong. Outsiders then either reject the culture or the culture rejects them.

4. Managed Evolution by Aligning Critical Subcultures

If the founder's beliefs are well adapted to the environmental realities that the new organization faces, it grows and ages. With growth and aging come several new organizational phenomena. Strong subunits arise based on function, geography, markets, or products, and these subunits have to survive in their various external environments. Thus, in adapting to these external environments they evolve beliefs and assumptions that are congruent with but different from the core assumptions of the founder. Such subcultures are often called "silos" or "stove pipes" if they reflect functions, products, markets, or geographies. The boundaries they build around themselves make it harder to communicate across them and integrate their various efforts.

But this is not the only kind of subculture that forms. With age, each set of employees and managers at a given level within the organization also shares common experiences that become the basis for mutually held assumptions about how things are and how they should be done. The shared assumptions of employees differ from those of management, especially if workers are unionized—and particularly so if they belong to an international union. First-line supervisors develop shared assumptions based on the nature of their jobs. Staff groups such as engineering, finance, and planning develop their own subcultures based on their professional and occupational backgrounds. Middle managers develop subcultures based on the similarities of their roles. Perhaps most important of all, CEOs and the people they take into their confidence discover that they live in a very complex financial world that only other CEOs really understand, thus creating yet another subculture that must be aligned with the others in the organization.

It is especially crucial to understand the three generic subcultures of *operations* (the line and sales organization), *engineering* (the designers of products, processes, and organizational structures) and *top management* (the CEO and his or her confidants) because they exist in all kinds of organizations in some form and are potentially in conflict with each other.[3] Especially engineering and top management have as their primary reference group—the group to which members compare themselves—outside the organization in their respective occupational communities. Thus, for engineers and other organizational designers it is the design profession that dictates many of the values and assumptions they live by. They are likely to share assumptions that perfect designs are free of people and that it is people who make mistakes and should be engineered out of processes as much as possible. The subculture of engineering and design, then, is potentially in conflict with various operator, line, and sales units that depend on people and teamwork for effective performance.

In the case of CEOs, it is their board, the financial markets, the analyst community, and fellow CEOs in the industry that define their environment and thereby create some of the assumptions that CEOs learn to live by. However much they believe that people are important, their job demands primary attention to the financial affairs of the organization; inevitably, people come to be seen as a cost factor. In practice, the CEO subculture is also out of sync with the engineering subculture because of the latter's desire to build the most elegant system, which is usually too costly. Hence the degree to which these occupational subcultures are aligned with each other is a major determinant of how well the organization as a whole functions.

In your role as a leader you have to understand that each of these subcultures is necessary for the total effectiveness of the organization and, therefore, that they must be aligned with each other. Effective evolution, in this case, requires the nurturing of each of these subcultures. It does not help the organization if each subculture believes the others are dysfunctional. Your job as a culture change agent in a young and growing organization is to develop meetings and events in which enough mutual understanding can arise among them to enable each to flourish and grow. Some of the processes that have to be used in multinational cross-cultural groups apply here as well, and these will be described in greater detail in Chapter Ten.

The Impact of Size and Age—Bureaucratization and the Loss of "Functional Familiarity"

When differentiation into various kinds of subcultures occurs in a small organization where everyone knows everyone else, the communication difficulties that might arise during coordination efforts can be resolved informally. People are "functionally familiar" with each other in that they know one another's working styles, what verbal commitments mean, the time horizons that are used, and generally how to calibrate each other. With increasing organizational size, people can no longer remain functionally familiar with others, so they have to resort to more formal processes of contracting, monitoring each other, and in general substituting processes and procedures for personal contact.

When DEC was small a hardware engineer could go to the software department and ask whether the supporting software would be ready in six months so that the product could be launched. The software manager would say, "Sure." The hardware manager would then tell me that he "knew" that this meant nine months because "he is always a bit optimistic but he will get it done, so I can plan accordingly." As DEC became large and more differentiated, the same scenario would no longer produce the same result. The software manager would again say, "Sure," but the hardware manager would tell me that he was unsure whether that meant six months, nine months, twelve months, or never, because some other priorities might bump his project. The software manager was now a stranger, embedded in other organizational units, someone with an unknown personality. The hardware manager now had to resort to getting a written commitment so that he could hold the software manager to it. Bureaucracy was born.

As deals have to be negotiated with strangers, trust levels erode, and political processes begin to replace teamwork in pursuit of common goals. The subunits become power centers, and their leaders become barons with an increasingly local agenda. Echelons of supervision, midlevel management, and senior management develop their own norms and force the communications going up and down the hierarchy into certain forms. For example, engineers learn that they have to put their design ideas into cost-benefit language to get middle management to look at proposals, and middle management learns that it has to show the benefits of the project in terms of the particular financial issues the CEO is grappling with at the time.[4]

For as long as the founders or founding families retain ownership and control, they can function as the integrating force and use some of the basic assumptions of the culture as the primary integrating and control mechanisms. Charismatic founder-owners can continue to be the glue by articulating the values and principles they expect organization management to follow. But with continuing success, the impact of size and age makes this form of coordination harder to implement. The inability of founders to let go increases the danger that dysfunctional elements of the culture will be perpetuated and that new managers with adaptively appropriate assumptions and values will not be permitted to gain power. How succession is managed then becomes a major issue for the survival of the organization.

Managing Problems of Succession

Succession from founders and owning families to mid-life under general managers involves a number of sub-phases and processes. How companies actually move from being under the domination of a founder or family to the state of being managed by second-, third-, and fourth-generation general managers has so many variants that one can only identify some prototypical processes and events.

The first-and often most critical-of these processes is the shift from the founder to the next CEO, whether a family member or an outsider. Even if this person is the founder's son, daughter, or other trusted family member, it is in the nature of founder-entrepreneurs to have difficulty giving up what they have created. In extreme cases, founders may be unconsciously willing even to destroy their organization to prove to the world how indispensable they were. On the other hand, some entrepreneurs whose passion is to keep creating new ventures find it easy to go public and step down or turn successful ventures over to friends and colleagues.

During the transition phase, conflict over which elements of the culture employees like or do not like reflects what they do or do not like about the founder, since most of the culture is likely to be a playing out of the founder's personality. Battles develop between "conservatives," who like the founding culture, and "liberals" or "radicals," who want to change the culture (partly because they want to enhance their own power positions). The danger in this situation is that feelings about the founder are projected onto the culture and, in the effort to displace the leader, much of the culture comes under challenge. If members of the organization forget that the culture is a set of learned solutions that have produced success, comfort, and identity, then they may try to change the very things they value and need.

Often missing in this phase is understanding of what the culture is and what it is doing for the organization, regardless of how it came to be. Succession processes must therefore be designed to enhance those parts of the culture that provide identity, distinctive competence, and protection from anxiety. Such a process can probably be managed only from within, because an outsider could not possibly understand the subtleties of the cultural issues and the emotional relationships between founders and employees.

Preparation for succession is usually psychologically difficult both for the founder and for potential successors because entrepreneurs typically like to maintain a high level of control. They may officially be grooming successors, but unconsciously they may be preventing powerful and competent people from functioning in these roles. Or they may designate successors but prevent them from having enough responsibility to learn how to do the job—what we might call the Prince Albert syndrome, remembering that Queen Victoria did not permit her son many opportunities to practice being king. This pattern is particularly likely to operate with a father-to-son transition as was well illustrated in the history of IBM.[5]

When senior management or the founder confronts the criteria for a successor, cultural issues are forced into the open. It is now clear that much of the culture has become an attribute and property of the organization, even though it may have started out as the property of the founder. If the founder or family is still dominant in the organization, one may expect little culture change but a great deal of effort to clarify, integrate, maintain, and evolve the culture, primarily because it is identified with the founder. Companies that have made successful transitions often differentiate the essential elements of their cultures, the cultural DNA so to speak, from more peripheral elements and attempt to ensure that the core is preserved. This is why hybrids are often the best successors—they maintain the core but evolve the periphery, as was the case of Watson Jr. maintaining IBM's marketing core but branching out into new areas of technology.

When the founder or family finally relinquishes control, formal management succession provides an opportunity to change the direction of the culture by finding the right kind of successor—a hybrid who represents what is needed for the organization to survive, yet is acceptable because he is "one of us" and therefore is also a conserver of parts of the old culture. In some companies, after several outsiders have failed as CEOs, someone is found who was with the company earlier and therefore perceived by the family to understand the company-even though he or she brought in many new assumptions about how to run the business, as was the case in the Jones company.

If the succession process is not managed effectively, founders and founding families lose power and are eventually replaced by formal means. If ownership becomes public, a board primarily made up of outsiders is created and a professional manager from outside the organization becomes the CEO. As family influence declines and the board goes on appointing CEOs, organizations enter what I think of as their mid-life. As we shall see, the culture issues in mid-life are quite different.

In terms of the change and learning model, the key issue is whether or not the young organization is able to perceive relevant disconfirming information. Because the culture is the glue and the source of identity, commitment to the culture also acts as a filter against disconfirming information. An example of this process in the case of DEC was the inability to perceive that the scientific market that valued DEC's product innovation was shrinking in relation to the growing personal computer market that wanted simple turnkey commodity products. DEC kept "paying attention to its customers" but was not taking into account that this customer base was growing much more slowly than the other one. Therefore, DEC's rationalization that "growth would take care of current areas of excess of people and projects" proved to be a fatal blind spot. The consequence was that DEC never launched a culture change project of the sort that would have been needed to change the economics of the firm. Instead, the culture of innovation was so highly valued and so strong that economic criteria were sacrificed.

The Bottom Line

Cultural growth and evolution is managed by the leadership of a young organization through different mechanisms. In the founding and early development stage, cultural assumptions define the group's identity and distinctive competence and hence are strongly held. If leaders detect maladaptive assumptions, the only way they can change culture is to bias the normal evolutionary processes, or produce therapeutic interventions that give group members new insight and thereby allow them to evolve their culture more manageably. The other major mechanism available to leaders in this stage is to locate and systematically promote hybrids in the organization who represent the main elements of the culture but who have learned some other assumptions in various subgroups that are considered adaptive.

The transition to mid-life is fraught with cultural issues because succession problems force cultural assumptions out into the open. Group members are likely to confuse elements of the culture with elements of the founder's personality, and subgroups are likely to form for or against some of what the founder stands for. Cultural issues thus become salient during the transition of succession, but the change mechanisms are likely to be the same as the ones I have described, unless in the transition the company is sold or taken over by completely new management, in which case a new culture formation process begins.

The key issue for culture change leaders is that they must become sufficiently marginal in their own culture to recognize what may be its strengths worth preserving and its maladaptive assumptions requiring change. This demands the ability to perceive disconfirming information and to use it to define new kinds of behavior so that adaptive learning and change processes can be launched. This process is especially difficult for entrepreneurial founders because the early success of their organization is likely to make them believe that their own assumptions are ultimately the correct ones.

Questions for the Reader

If you are in a young organization, ask yourself what the non-negotiable values that you would not care to give up are.

- Why do you hold on to these values?
- Where did they come from?
- Will they help your organization to succeed in the future?

If you are not in a young organization, locate someone who is and ask him or her these questions.

8

CULTURE DYNAMICS IN THE MATURE COMPANY

Organizational mid-life or maturity creates a series of cultural issues that differ dramatically from the issues of growth and early evolution. As I pointed out in the last chapter, during the growth period the emphasis is on building, evolving, consolidating, stabilizing, and institutionalizing the cultural elements that work. Values and assumptions become embedded in organizational structures and processes. As organizations reach maturity, a wholly different set of issues arise because if change is needed, we are now dealing with *unlearning* and replacing assumptions and values in a system of highly differentiated subcultures that are likely to be both functional in some parts and dysfunctional in other parts. All the mechanisms of change referred to in the previous chapter still apply, but new mechanisms now have to be developed because the management structures in mature organizations are different from those of founder-led and founder-owned organizations.

From Ownership to General Management Structures

The most salient characteristic of organizational mid-life is that the management processes are now created by promoted general managers, not entrepreneurs, founders, or founding families. When the founding family is no longer in an ownership or dominant position, or after at least two generations of general management, or when the organization has grown in size to the point at which the sheer number of non-family managers overweighs the family members, we are talking about mid-life and maturity.

In building their businesses, founders and founding families often hold values other than purely economic ones. David Packard was quoted as saying that "It should be possible to run a business in a gentlemanly fashion" and he always stood for the "HP way" as being highly oriented toward employees (not just stockholders). Ken Olsen at one time said that he was reluctant to open too many plants in Maine because it would alter the economic and social structure of that state, even though there would be economic advantages to having plants there. Founders impose non-economic values on the organization and embed them in the culture.

On the other hand, general managers who have worked their way up in the organization usually learn that humanistic, social, environmental, spiritual, and other non-economic values have to be subordinated to the pragmatic problems of running the business and keeping it financially viable. Promoted managers do not have the luxury that founder-owners enjoy of taking financial risks to preserve certain of their values and beliefs. Promoted general managers are usually more vulnerable to powerful outside boards; they have shorter tenures and learn how to survive in organizations. As CEOs, they typically come into their jobs when the organization is already highly differentiated in terms of subcultures.

As such managers rise and take on greater responsibilities, they also discover the painful reality that managing systems and processes gradually displaces managing people. As one CEO of a consumer goods industry told me:

"I started out as a store manager, where I knew all of my people very well. When I was promoted to a district with ten stores, I visited all of the stores on a regular basis and still knew the several hundred people who worked in them. But then, when I was promoted to regional and eventually division manager, I discovered I could no longer know enough of the people in the stores to feel personally attached. I had to invent systems, procedures, and rules and implement them through my immediate subordinates. But at this stage it felt like a completely different kind of job and became much more impersonal. This was the most important transition in my managerial career."

This comment refers to the loss of "functional familiarity," which was pointed out in the last chapter as one of the most important consequences of organizational growth and age. Except for the immediate subordinates and a finite number of others the manager can remember, his or her relationships to people become more formal and process-driven. From a cultural perspective, the mid-life organization therefore faces a very complicated situation. It is established and must maintain itself through some kind of continued growth-and-renewal process. It must decide whether to pursue such growth through further geographical expansion, development of new products, opening up of new markets, vertical integration to improve its cost and resource positions, divisionalization, mergers and acquisitions, partnerships and joint ventures, or spin-offs. The past history of the organization's growth and development is not necessarily a good guide to what will succeed in the future because the environment is likely to change; more important, internal changes are likely to alter the organization's unique strengths and weaknesses. The embedded culture is, therefore, both a potential help and a potential hindrance in the further strategic development of the organization.

Whereas culture was a necessary glue in the period of growth, the most important elements of the culture are now deeply embedded in the structure and major processes of the organization. Hence, consciousness of the culture and deliberate attempts to build, integrate, or conserve the culture are less important. The culture that the organization acquired during its early years is now taken for granted and largely invisible. The only elements that are likely to be conscious are the credos, dominant espoused values, company slogans, written charters, and other public pronouncements of what the company wants to be and claims to stand for—its philosophy and ideology.

Whereas leadership created culture in the early stages, culture now creates leaders, in the sense that only those managers who fit the mold are promoted to top positions. In fact, one of the most dangerous aspects of culture at this stage is that *the shared tacit assumptions are now an unconscious determinant of most of what goes on in the organization, including even the mission and strategy of the organization.*

At this stage, it is more difficult to decipher the culture and make people aware of it because it is so embedded in routines. Raising awareness of the culture may even be counterproductive unless there is some crisis or specific problem to be solved. Managers view culture discussions as boring and irrelevant, especially if the company is large and well-established. On the other hand, if the organization undertakes geographical expansions, mergers and acquisitions, or joint ventures, and/or introduces new technologies, it must do a careful self-assessment to determine whether the existing culture is compatible with the new ways of thinking and behaving that are to be introduced.

Also at this stage, there may be strong forces toward cultural diffusion and loss of integration. Powerful subcultures have developed, and a highly integrated corporate culture may be difficult to maintain in a large, differentiated, geographically dispersed organization. Furthermore, as the organization ages, it becomes less clear whether all the subcultural units of an organization should be uniform and integrated. Several conglomerates I have worked with spent a good deal of time wrestling with the question of whether to attempt to preserve, or in some cases build, a common culture. Are the costs associated with such an effort worth it? Is there even a danger of imposing assumptions on a subunit that might not fit the situation at all? On the other hand, if subunits are all allowed to develop their own cultures, what is the competitive advantage of being a single organization? Resolving such questions often requires careful assessment of the actual culture to see what elements, if any, should be generalized, given the varying tasks of the organizational units.

From a cultural perspective, then, the essence of the leader's job is not how to create an organizational culture but how to manage the diversity of subcultural forces that are already operating; how to integrate and further evolve a highly differentiated organization; and how to enhance elements of the culture that are congruent with new environmental realities while changing dysfunctional elements of the culture. If cultural elements have to be changed, then we are dealing with transformative change, which requires mechanisms that go beyond the evolutionary ones characteristic of the young and growing organization.

Questions for the Reader

Spend a little time by yourself, or with some colleagues, reviewing the history of your organization.

- Think back to the founders. Ask what deep values and assumptions they held that became part of the culture of the organization. If necessary, locate some old-timers who remember what the founding culture was like.

- Identify powerful leaders who came after the founders. Ask yourself whether or not they changed elements of the culture during their leadership period. If yes, in what way? What new ways of thinking and behaving did they introduce?

- Now shift your focus to the environment. Ask yourself how the economic, technological, political, and social environments in which your company operates have changed. To what extent are some of the deepest assumptions of your founders and early leaders no longer functional in the present environment?

Culture Change Processes in Organizational Mid-Life: Planned and Managed Culture Change Through Parallel Learning Systems

The culture change mechanisms described in Chapter Seven—general and specific evolution, guided evolution through insight, managed evolution through promotion of hybrids, and empowering managers from selected subcultures—all continue to operate in mid-life. But because culture is now more differentiated and embedded, elements of the culture that are potentially dysfunctional require change processes that have to be more transformative than evolutionary. Change now involves *unlearning* old ways of thinking and old ways of behaving, a process that is fundamentally more threatening and that almost invariably creates resistance to change. Evolving the culture through systematic selection of managers from certain subcultures is often too slow a process to make the necessary transformations. The major change mechanism then becomes "planned and managed culture change," through a systematic process involving change leaders and change teams operating as parallel structures.

The actual change activities in a managed change program will vary according to the situation, but almost all such programs involve the creation of a "parallel learning system" in which some new assumptions are learned and tested.[1] The process starts with senior management experiencing enough disconfirmation to realize that a change process must be launched. Senior management also must realize that, if elements of the culture may require change, a temporary parallel structure will be needed because it is often too painful for everyone in the organization to give up a shared assumption in favor of an unknown substitute or to learn some new and untested behavior.

The essence of this concept is that some part of the organization must become marginal and expose itself to new ways of thinking so that it can be objective about the strengths and weaknesses of the existing cultural elements and examine how these will aid or hinder the changes to be made. Fully engaged insiders simply cannot see the culture in which they are embedded clearly enough to assess and evaluate its elements. For example, in the financial crisis of 2008, whether or not to give money to the ailing American auto industry hinged on an assessment of whether the current auto executives were capable of making the kinds of changes that would be required to make the industry internationally competitive and environmentally responsible. Skepticism about their ability to change arose from the fact that General Motors had successfully innovated with Saturn, with the electric car, and with the Fremont factory built on the Toyota model, yet had failed to utilize any of the insights from those innovations in their mainstream business.

On the other hand, having an entirely outside assessment of the culture is equally unlikely to be productive because the outsider does not know enough of the cultural nuances to be able to make an accurate assessment and will not have a sense of where there is leverage to begin the change process. The solution is to create a temporary parallel structure that includes key insiders who then work with outsiders or hybrids to decipher the culture and plan the change program. If some part of the organization can learn an alternative way of behaving and thinking, and if the alternative can be shown to work, then there is less anxiety as the alternative is gradually introduced into the main part of the organization. An excellent example of such a parallel system was the staff group that Procter & Gamble created to redesign their manufacturing process (referred to in Chapter One).

A current example is Alpha Power, a large urban power company, which was brought up on criminal charges fifteen years ago because it had allegedly concealed the existence of asbestos in one of its plants. The judge fined the company heavily, forced it to sign a consent order that put the company on probation for several years and said that "the culture" was part of the problem. He ordered periodic reviews of progress by outside consulting firms and appointed a monitor to keep close track of the company's progress in becoming more environmentally responsible. The monitor wrote quarterly reports highlighting both successes and failures in the company's efforts to become more responsible; the failures he cited and described in great detail created more disconfirmation and more survival anxiety throughout the organization.

One of the most stringent goals was to become more open and honest with the government in admitting environmental events and putting into place remedial measures. Senior management came to the important realization that, to be competitive in the future deregulated market, the kind of employee behavior that would lead to responsible behavior with respect to environment, health, and safety issues (EH&S) would also be desirable to make the company generally more effective.

The CEO strongly articulated a vision for employees to become more team-oriented, more open in their communications, more personally responsible, better at planning and risk assessment, and more capable of assessing and remedying EH&S issues. A senior vice president for environmental affairs was hired and charged with building an organization that would provide training, consulting, expertise in diagnosis and remediation, and—most important—some oversight to ensure that EH&S affairs were properly handled at every level. A high-level environmental committee (EHSC) including all of senior management was formed to meet monthly to assess progress in reducing environmental events, such as oil spills, set policy, and generally oversee the entire program.

In addition, an environmental quality review board (EQRB) was formed, consisting of two highly respected environmental lawyers whose job was to help the company with its problems of compliance. The board would also ensure that the program as it evolved would satisfy the U.S. attorney's office sufficiently to warrant recommendation that the probation be lifted at the end of the three-year period. I was added to this board as a "culture expert" when it became apparent from the monitor's quarterly reports that he viewed "the culture" of the company as being one of the major constraints to effective change in the EH&S area, but no one was quite sure of what he or others meant by "the culture." We were permanent members of the EHSC and represented the outsider point of view toward cultural analysis. The fact that this committee had outsiders as well as high-ranking insiders made it de facto the steering committee for the entire transformation effort and functioned as the parallel structure.

The Change Team and Change Steps

The group that functions as the parallel structure may or may not actually design and implement the change programs that will be needed. Often it become the "steering committee" with accountability and oversight, but the change team is usually a different group or actual subunit of a department that has to undertake the actual work of designing and implement the day-to-day assessment and change activities. These activities are best viewed as several necessary steps that have to be taken for the overall change to succeed. Many models have been proposed for what these steps need to be and of these, the most useful one was developed by Beckhard and Harris (1987) as shown in Figure 8.1.

Some of these five steps require very little time, while others are themselves whole programs, but no step should be bypassed. Although this process model applies to any kind of change, it is especially relevant to changes that may involve the culture because it enables you to determine the optimal time for culture assessment and analysis. How this works in practice is illustrated in the Alpha Power culture change program.

Step 1. Why Change?

The first step is to determine whether change is, in fact, necessary and feasible. Disconfirmation has created survival anxiety or guilt, leading to a lot of turmoil and proposed action, new visions, and calls for solutions. At some point internal and

Figure 8.1. A Map of the Change Management Process

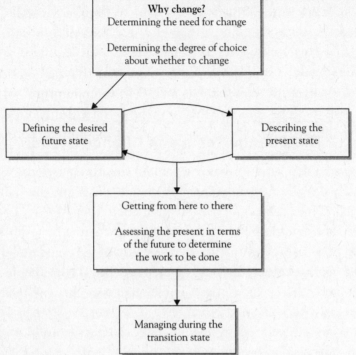

Adapted from Beckhard and Harris, 1987.

external disconfirming forces have created enough survival anxiety or guilt for leaders to have concluded that change was necessary and have created the change team. It is important for the change team to review and reaffirm the prior actions to ensure that the disconfirming data are valid and that the launching of a change program actually makes sense.

In the case of Alpha Power, the steering committee (EHSC) empowered the vice president of environmental affairs and his entire organization to become the change team and to work with line management to implement various change processes. All our discussions reaffirmed the need for change and reinforced the concept that fixing the environmental problems would actually improve the overall management of the organization.

The change planning was to be done with that larger goal in mind. The program now rested not only on the external disconfirmation but also on the internal desire to improve overall. The environmental program would, in a sense, be a pilot for a more general improvement effort.

To begin the change program in earnest, the vice president of environmental affairs created a "culture committee" whose role was to think specifically about how the culture of Alpha would impact the change program. This committee consisted of a diagonal slice of the organization to ensure that subcultures would be adequately represented in any assessment process.

Step 2. What Is the Ideal Future State?

If a change is needed and is deemed possible, the next step for senior management and the change committee is to define the ideal future state. This may have already been articulated and announced by leaders in the organization, but the change team must reassess the concept and ensure that the new vision is clear and behaviorally specific. The vision of the ideal future state should answer this question: "If we are successful in making the changes, what should our *behavior* look like in the future?"

Being very specific and concrete in terms of ideal new behavior does not come easily. In the case of Alpha, senior management said that the workers were to "become more environmentally responsible," that "communication in the future should be more open," and that "there should be more teamwork in the future." These were still very vague goals that did not specify precise behavior. One of my roles as the outsider at this point was to probe just what leaders meant by these three goals. I found the following meanings:

- *"Responsibility"* meant that all workers were to feel responsible for identifying, reporting, and remediating any environmental spill, no matter how small, and take appropriate action.

- *"More open communication"* meant that, when an environmental event was identified, the employee was to report it to the relevant environmental agencies within a specified time. No more covering up or dawdling on reporting.

- *"More teamwork"* meant that if employees saw other employees ignoring or failing to report an environmental event, they were to speak to that employee, get him or her to change, and, if not successful, to report him or her to the supervisor.

Only when the vision of the future was stated to this degree of specificity could Alpha raise the questions to itself: What about our culture? Will it help or hinder? What needs to change? The culture now finally comes into explicit consciousness around the assessment of the present state.

Steps 3 and 4. Assessing the Present State and Planning

Once the ideal state is well understood, the change team must diagnose and assess the present state of the system to determine what the gaps are between the ideal future and the present. In assessing the present state, it is especially important to create a parallel system to ensure objectivity. A change team of all insiders is likely to misperceive the state of the culture or not perceive it at all because team members are so embedded in it.

The cultural assessment processes described earlier in Chapter Five are appropriate and necessary at this point. If the culture is assessed before the ideal future state is known, it is likely to be diffuse, boring, and useless. If the culture assessment is done at this stage, it should reveal where there are gaps and potential barriers to achieving the vision and the concrete goals derived from it. At this point the change process also moves from analysis and assessment to concrete planning. For each of the gaps identified, specific plans must now be made for what to do next, how to get from the present to the future.

In Alpha Power both the EHSC and the culture committee spent a great deal of time on this stage to identify what the current norms in the organization were that would aid or hinder getting to the new behavior.

Step 5. Managing the Transition

The change model described in Chapter Six provides a useful tool for planning the details of the change process called "force field analysis." With respect to every behavior that has been identified as the future ideal, one can take the present behavior and ask: "What 'driving forces' exist in the current organization toward the future behavior we want?" These can be listed on the left side of a sheet of paper. On the right side of the paper can be listed the "restraining forces" that prevent the behavior from occurring. For example, the timely reporting of spills is clearly driven by management pressure, the threat of discipline for failing to report, the employee's own motivation to be responsible, and many other forces. On the restraining side might be ignorance of what an oil spill is (it might just be water or something that will dry up quickly), how small a quantity needs to be reported, time pressure to get on with other parts of the job, inconvenience, supervisors encouraging the employee to forget about it, group norms that employees should not have to do that sort of thing, and a self-image of that not being part of the job.

Some of the behavioral goals seemed on the face of it to be directly contradictory to the basic job employees had. For example, in the old way of working, if a hospital transformer broke down and the work crew dispatched to fix it discovered that their truck was leaking oil into a nearby sewer, there was no question that they would fix the transformer first and then worry about the oil spill later. In the new way of working, they were required to do both, something that seemed impossible. To give another example, in the old way of working, if one member of a work crew was not wearing safety equipment or was doing something unsafe, crewmates would say nothing, even if it endangered them. In the new way of working, they were supposed to be mutually responsible and monitor each other, something that seemed equally impossible given the group norms.

Movement toward the new way of working is then produced by changing the balance in the force field, either by increasing the driving forces or reducing the restraining forces. Depending on how the culture assessment came out, cultural norms and assumptions are likely to appear on *both* the driving and restraining force sides. The driving forces include the disconfirming information that causes survival anxiety and one of the main restraining forces will be what I have called "learning anxiety."

No change will occur unless the driving forces (the survival anxiety) are greater than the restraining forces (the learning anxiety). The change team then needs to examine each set of forces to determine what to focus the change program on in terms of access, feasibility, cost, and desirability. For example, severe disciplinary measures for any cases of failing to report are an obvious way to increase survival anxiety. On the other hand, that might increase union resistance and lead to a deterioration of relations. Or it might be discovered that one of the reason for failure to report was that supervisors were encouraging covering up, in which case punishing the employee would be counterproductive. One might then realize that supervisory pressure to cover up is one of the restraining forces and that one should try to reduce it by shifting pressure to supervisors and encouraging employees to speak up, even if supervisors discouraged it.

In general it will be found, as was pointed out in Chapter Six, that the optimal way to produce change, is to *reduce the restraining forces*, the learning anxiety, by providing psychological safety during and after the learning process. This means involving the learner, providing training, role models, resources, and supportive rewards and incentives.

For example, an obvious source of learning anxiety in Alpha Power was lack of information and knowledge about environmental hazards. If employees were to identify and clean up environmental spills, asbestos, mercury, PCBs, and other hazardous substances, they had to know what to look for in the streets, in building basements, in the various chemical and electrical processes they worked with. All of the employees had to be educated and specifically trained.

By the time I arrived on the scene, most of this training had already occurred because Alpha Power had a highly developed learning center in which all technical training for their highly hazardous technology took place. The strongly autocratic, paternalistic, and technical cultural assumptions that dominated the culture had already been put to good use in getting the employee population up to speed on the technical side of environmental compliance. These same cultural elements drove the reward and discipline system and made it very clear, for example, that any supervisor or employee who encouraged covering up an environmental event or harassed another employee for wanting to report something was subject to severe discipline, including termination.

More problematic was the cultural restraining force of employees thinking of themselves as keeping on the power and solving emergency power problems, not as cleaners. The vision of the future did not jibe well with the self-image that many employees held, as was illustrated above with the hospital generator example. To deal with this, all the levels of management and supervision had to have insight into the issue and develop positive messages to facilitate this change in self-image.

The vice president of EHS working with me and the two environmental lawyers (the EQRB) used the Culture Committee to begin to think through how to use cultural insight to evolve this crucial cultural element. This committee and several subcommittees articulated as best they could the detailed programs that would help to achieve the change goals and overcome the barriers to achieving the desired future state.

It was decided after several months that I should make a presentation to the EHSC, which would begin to educate them on the concept of culture. The essence of a good educational intervention is to get difficult concepts across concretely so that the audience can apply the theory to themselves immediately. The presentation was discussed at length, and senior management began to appreciate how complex this change would be. Most important, I needed to test whether or not the group was still committed to culture change, given better understanding of what would be involved. They asserted that they were committed and followed up the assertion by scheduling a similar talk for the next layer of management below them. In the meantime, I continued to meet with groups that would help define what the cultural dilemma was at the employee level. In other words, if a new way of working were to be defined, what in the old way of working would get in the way? These elements of the culture gradually surfaced during the group interviews we held with employees.

In terms of making employees responsible, the culture aided the process because of strong organizational traditions of training employees thoroughly and enforcing new behavior through a strong autocratic paternalism. The need for quicker upward communication was also aided by a well-engrained discipline system. However, employees "ratting on each other" clearly was out of line with the strong union subculture. The vice president of EHS also discovered from actual experience that the deep paternalistic assumption of not firing people led to a dysfunctional career system where less competent employees and managers tended to be "parked" until retirement in areas like environment and safety.

The parts of the culture that I found hardest to deal with were certain elements of the employee and union subcultures. There was a strong norm to keep dirty linen in the work group. If reporting a spill was embarrassing because it resulted from negligence or an error, this would be a strong restraining force against reporting. If a fellow employee failed to report or did something environmentally harmful, there was a strong norm to respect that employee's independence and not do anything. The strong tradition of paternalistic autocracy created the norm that if a supervisor asked employees to do something that broke rules, they would do what they were asked to do.

Inasmuch as these were norms based in strong groups, the only way to accomplish change in this area was to involve all echelons of the organization, especially the employees themselves. If they did not participate actively in defining the methods of learning, their norms would not change. To support the whole program and to begin the involvement of employees, a number of structural interventions were made.

Structural and Process Interventions

Some of these changes had been made early in the program because they reflected the stable elements of the culture—strong hierarchy, deference to superiors, paternalism, an implicit promise of lifetime employment, and a commitment to as much education and training as would be needed to work responsibly and safely. I list here all of the changes that were made in the first several years of the program.

- A senior vice president for environmental affairs was hired.
- Environmental managers were placed in each operating unit and given authority to determine how EH&S-related work was to be performed.
- Detailed procedures for identifying and remediating environmental hazards were developed and published.
- Intensive training programs on these procedures for supervisors and employees were launched.
- Strong disciplinary procedures were instituted to punish supervisors or fellow employees who harassed anyone reporting to the court-appointed monitor.
- Public recognition and awards were given to employees who demonstrated environmental responsibility and invented new procedures for heightening both efficiency and environmental responsibility.

- New technologies were created to aid in dealing with oil spills and other problems.
- Detailed measurement systems were instituted to track the rate of environmental incidents.
- The EHS oversight committees met monthly to monitor the whole program.
- The auditing department investigated all EH&S incidents to determine root cause and other causal factors, and to build a database from which generalizations about EH&S issues could be made.

Involving the Employees

The structural interventions mentioned above were necessary, but not sufficient. Employees and their union had to become involved in the environmental issues because the identification and dealing with hazardous material was a safety issue as well. Central to this involvement program was the invitation to the elected leader of the union to join the top-management steering committee. He and one or more other union officials now regularly attend the monthly meetings and have become active participants in the key decisions around the EH&S issues.

Labor/Management Safety Committees

In each major unit of Alpha, a joint safety committee was created to identify safety and environmental issues and, if appropriate, to develop procedures for dealing with them. For example, one of those committees figured out that the solution to the hospital generator/truck oil leak problem was to put buckets of sand and protective blankets on *every* truck so that if it was discovered to be leaking upon arrival at the hospital, the spill would be contained, the generator fixed, and the spill then cleaned up. Once this procedure was adopted, employees wondered why, in retrospect, it had seemed so "impossible" to do this.

The Time-Out Program

One geographical subunit of Alpha realized that it had always been a company policy to "stop a job" if an environmental or safety issue was detected, but there was no easy mechanism for an employee to actually do it. The group realized that the employee needed a tool, a concrete way of calling a "time out." Each employee was issued a small green card with instructions to call time out whenever he or she felt that to proceed would involve some EH&S risk. The job would then have to be stopped until an EH&S expert could assess the situation and give directions on what to do next.

Needless to say, considerable anxiety developed in the management ranks because of the possibility that employees would use "time out" frivolously or irresponsibly, but that has not happened. In those cases in which an employee did stop a job, it was found that expert help was indeed needed, and new procedures were instituted. The program was so successful in this one unit that the company eventually made it a general program throughout and gave it senior management's blessing and support.

Notice that "time out" is a concrete way of changing the hierarchical norms of the culture by giving employees the license to stop a job, which means refusing to continue to do what the supervisor had sanctioned or even explicitly ordered. Notice also that the old norm of always following orders is now undermined, but the new norm of "we have the power and the responsibility to stop a job when necessary" is not yet totally accepted. A new culture has not formed; only new behavior has been sanctioned. Forming a new cultural element depends on whether the new behavior is, in the long run, successful in making the company more responsible and productive. In the meantime, acceptance of this program by supervisors is a clear signal that the old hierarchical culture is gradually evolving toward some employee empowerment around EH&S issues.

Union Safety Committees

The new way of working was getting more clear in the environmental area, but it remained a problem in the safety area because of the norm of not ratting out or confronting your buddies. The vision was clear: good safety requires teamwork, and it is the responsibility of every member of the team to be sure every other member is following safety procedures. If one member is not wearing a safety helmet or safety glasses, it is the responsibility of the other team members to point this out and demand compliance. But this means abandoning the implicit heroic model of getting the job done through individual heroic behavior, as well as abandoning the norm that each employee has autonomy in deciding what to wear or not wear.

To deal with this dilemma, it is again necessary to look for creative examples within the organization. One came from a department in which the labor management safety committee decided that safety inspections and post-accident reviews should not be done solely by safety experts but rather by employees who were peers in rank. If a fellow employee from another group points out to a given workgroup the "stupidity" of not wearing safety equipment, this clearly has more impact than if the message comes from the supervisor or a staff expert. In some departments it was decided that the safety inspectors who would visit jobs should be union members rather than safety experts or managers. They received the relevant training and have had more success in getting fellow employees to wear their personal protective equipment.

Employee Involvement in Equipment Redesign

Another example comes from a group in which some engineers found that the safety equipment was cumbersome and uncomfortable. Instead of the traditional approach of "training" employees to use the existing equipment, they launched an employee group to redesign the equipment with the specific goal of making it usable in the particular working conditions they typically face. This process of redesign by employees themselves has proven to be successful in a number of areas.

The Way We Work Task Force

As certain norms evolved for both the environmental and safety work, an effort was made to institutionalize these norms through a high-level committee launched by the company president to articulate the norms as principles and to create task forces to evolve each of these principles into programs that would permeate the entire company. Inasmuch as one of these principles was to "strive for perpetual improvement" and another one was to "celebrate success," the task forces not only sought out good examples in different units, but then nominated these for the special honor of presenting their particular accomplishment to senior management in a monthly award lunch. These monthly lunches at which four groups were honored at each lunch became a ritual symbolizing an important element of the "new culture."

It should also be noted that under the principle of perpetual improvement all kinds of other programs could be factored into the overall change program. Thus programs of conflict resolution, Six Sigma, re-engineering, quality circles, and employee surveys all would be seen as elements or components of the overall change program, rather than change mechanisms in their own right.

The Bottom Line

The new way of thinking and working involved using elements of the culture that aided the change process and confronting elements that stood in the way. To change elements involved all of the steps described in Chapter Six, especially "How Do You Create Psychological Safety?" That hinged on deep involvement of the employees who most feel the impact of the change, especially if employee norms are involved. Such norms cannot be changed by managerial fiat. Only the group can decide to abandon a given norm and begin to think along different lines.

As can be seen from this long example, the mid-life culture change process involves many steps and is, in a sense, never finished. As some processes are institutionalized and become stable, other sources of disconfirmation arise that launch new change initiatives. As some elements of the culture change, others are reinforced. For example, with more employee and union involvement, the tight hierarchy is evolving into more of a delegation style, but the absolute commitment to training is being reinforced. As the goals change from environmental responsibility to more emphasis on safety, the peer group norms become more of a focus for change programs to evolve from individual autonomy to employees caring for each other.

The triggers for mid-life culture change will be highly variable for different organizations, but the mechanism by which the culture will evolve will always be some form of the planned change program that has been described—the creation of a parallel system, a functioning change team, and a five-step change process.

Questions for the Reader

Think about a personal or organizational change program that you have experienced and see whether you can identify the activities that were involved in each of the five basic steps of the change program.

- Did you create a parallel system to help diagnose how the culture would aid or hinder the change?
- Did you identify the change targets in specific behavioral terms?
- Did the culture aid or hinder you in making the change?
- What lessons did you learn that would influence how you would design and manage a future change program?

9

MID-LIFE CRISIS AND POTENTIAL DECLINE

One of the persistent questions about culture is whether a strong culture is or is not an advantage in terms of effectiveness. This question now has to be revisited in terms of the stage of evolution of the organization. As I noted in Chapter Seven, in the growth stage, the strength of culture is both a goal and an advantage. Strong cultures provide a source of identity and control in that the members of the organization think alike, making it less necessary for formal control procedures to be instituted. However, with growth comes differentiation, the loss of functional familiarity, and the necessity for formal control procedures. As subcultures form the concept of strength loses its meaning, unless one is referring to some of the *core* assumptions of the corporate culture, the cultural DNA so to speak.

A strong culture in terms of *core* elements continues to be an advantage, but strength across all the many elements of the culture is now not only difficult to define but of questionable value. A more appropriate principle might be that the core elements of *each subculture* must be strong; but the notion of total corporate culture strength ceases to have meaning as the functioning of the organization increasingly depends on all of its different elements being effective in their own local environments. In fact, subculture *diversity* itself becomes a strength in that it affords different adaptive paths as the environment changes.

In this chapter we have to confront the further question of what happens when with growth and age strong *core assumptions of the corporate culture* become dysfunctional.

Changing Dysfunctional Elements
in the Core Culture

Continued success creates strongly held shared assumptions, and thus a strong corporate culture core. If the internal and external environments remain stable, this continues to be an advantage. However, if there is a change in the environment, some of those shared core assumptions can become liabilities, *precisely because of their strength*. Several circumstances can cause this problem:

First, the organization may no longer able to grow because it has saturated its markets and/or the industry has excess capacity. Ciba-Geigy faced this issue in its industrial chemicals market, forcing dramatic downsizing.

Second, patents may run out creating new economic conditions for the organization. As Ciba-Geigy's patents ran out, it discovered for the first time some of its inefficiencies in their production methods, forcing a dramatic cost-cutting program.

Third, the market standardizes on a commodity version of the products, causing all the producers to have to compete on price; the cost of innovation now becomes a major issue, as DEC discovered when the number of customers who were willing to pay for innovative products shrank in relation to the rapid growth of turnkey users.

Fourth, technological innovations can make the products obsolete and the core culture may not value the kinds of adaptive innovations that would be needed to stay viable.

Fifth, new leaders come into the organization who do not share or value the core assumptions on which the organization was built. This can result either from the departure of the key culture carriers and the inability to find replacements with the same values and assumptions, or because the board wants to change the core culture and deliberately brings in outsiders with different values and assumptions.

If the *core* or more central elements of the culture become dysfunctional, normal or even managed evolution of the kind described in the last chapters becomes irrelevant because at this stage senior leaders are themselves emotionally resistant to accepting the need for change. It takes unusually strong disconfirming forces to shake this emotional resistance and denial. Often it is only outside forces from economic downturns, scandals, legal actions, or board activity that breaks through and starts a change process. What then can be done?

The size of the organization does not matter, but age and developmental history do matter because they determine the strength of the core cultural elements. If an organization has a long history of success with certain assumptions about itself and the environment, it is unlikely to want to challenge or reexamine them. Even if those assumptions are brought to consciousness, the members of the organization are likely to want to hold on to them because they justify the past and are a source of pride and self-esteem. Such assumptions now operate as filters, making it difficult for key managers to understand and/or accept alternative strategies for survival and renewal.

A current example is the as-yet-unclear situation of the U.S. auto industry. It is evident that one of the core assumptions driving General Motors' culture was financial—one must always maximize the profit margin. Cars such as the Saturn or the electric car that moved toward better gas mileage were abandoned in favor of higher-margin SUVs. No amount of disconfirming data about the success of more fuel-efficient Japanese cars was accepted as requiring a change. Also at the core was the assumption that the only way to build cars was with a tight command-and-control structure. The Saturn experiment showed that a car could be efficiently built on a much more collaborative model, resembling the Scandinavian models of autonomous work groups, but this experiment never migrated to other parts of the organization.

Interestingly, in the 1970s we tested various groups of managers on their commitment to Theory Y (see the discussion of McGregor's theory in Chapter Four). Managers from U.S. auto companies had some of the lowest scores on this dimension, reflecting high Theory X scores (an assumed lack of faith in human desire to work and to commit to organizational goals). A study of organizational learning in one of the other major car companies showed that a design team organized more collaboratively could speed up the design and cut the costs by a very large amount, yet senior management neither understood the process innovations that the team had adopted nor tried to reproduce this model in other projects.[1]

The main point is that, if the disconfirming data challenge core cultural assumptions, those data tend to be ignored, denied, and/or rationalized away. Outside consultants can be brought in to show how the present culture will no longer be viable and to propose clear alternatives. But no matter how clear and persuasive the consultant tries to be, some alternatives are not even understood if they do not fit the core elements, the DNA of the culture. Even if they are understood, they will be denied or rationalized away because they create too much *learning* anxiety. This seems paradoxical because the disconfirmation produces a lot of survival anxiety. But if core elements of the culture are disconfirmed, the real problem is either the inability to even imagine what some genuinely new way of working might be or the outright rejection of it as undoable or undesirable.

As previously cited, a vivid example in DEC was its inability to develop a product to compete effectively with the IBM PC. All of senior management recognized that DEC should be in the PC market, but they tacitly assumed that the sophisticated user was their prime target. This assumption, in combination with the core assumption that "the market should decide," led to building three versions of the PC, all of them too elegant, too expensive, and still too complicated to use. The engineers were completely embedded in their traditional assumptions about the nature of computers and the marketplace. They believed they were designing a truly competitive product and were surprised that all three versions failed in the marketplace.

Possible Change Mechanisms

In a situation in which growth has slowed and decline is imminent, there are basically only two mechanisms of changing core cultural assumptions:

1. *Bankruptcy/Turnaround*: Destroying parts of the culture core and starting with a new management to build new behavior patterns that are more adaptive and that might then start a new culture creation process; or

2. *Merger/Acquisition*: Destroying the organization and its culture through a process of total reorganization via merger or acquisition

In either case, strong new change managers or transformational leaders are likely to be needed to unfreeze the organization and launch the change programs.[2] The human cost is always high, as the new managers discover that changing core cultural assumptions can only be accomplished quickly by simply getting rid of or forcing out the people who are the carriers of the old core assumptions.

There is no formula or program for this level of culture change. However, by looking at two examples in some detail, one can begin to infer some of the ways in which organizations can and do cope when core cultural assumptions are no longer viable. We will look first at a moderate change in Ciba-Geigy that preserved most of the elements of the culture while changing one critical element in the core and then look at a more drastic change, which destroyed several core elements and the organization itself, the case of DEC.

Moderate Core Culture Change in Ciba-Geigy

Ciba-Geigy (C-G) illustrates well a case in which a core assumption had to change, but where other elements of the culture mostly aided the turnaround process that was necessitated by economic and technological forces. In the late 1970s the chemical sector had overcapacity and needed to be downsized, while the pharmaceutical sector needed to become much more profitable relative to its competitors. As mentioned before, the geographical units and divisions of C-G had already become lean, but the Basel headquarters had not gotten rid of much of its overhead; the line units were pressuring headquarters for this to happen.

Making Pharma more efficient fell within the normal process of organizational improvement, but the downsizing of headquarters required the abandonment of a core cultural assumption in the human resources area, namely that C-G was a lifetime employer, totally committed to job security and would, therefore, never have a layoff. The prospect of having to lay people off was especially difficult in the headquarters city, where paternalism and nepotism had been accepted human resource practices.

The situation was defined by leadership as a "turnaround" but the actual three-year program also fits very well the managed change model described in the last chapter. A task force of senior managers functioning as a steering committee and a parallel system decided on twenty-five separate projects that would have to be done to achieve the vision of what the C-G of the future had to be. These projects covered all aspects of improvement of current processes, cost reduction, recombinations of technologies, and downsizing, especially in the chemical sector and in headquarters.

Small groups of senior executives then went to each of the units, explaining in detail what had to be done, and offering resources. At these meetings, the vision of the future ideal state was forcefully communicated and the personal presence of senior executives made it clear that the goals were nonnegotiable. This was to be a serious turnaround. Each project had a manager and linkage to a board member who monitored and oversaw the project. The steering committee met monthly to track progress and intervene where necessary. A three-year timetable was mandated for the changes to occur.

Each project group then had to design its own transformative change process to meet its objectives within the three-year time frame. For example, in a number of divisions it was observed that inefficient production processes had survived because of patent protection. As the patents ran out, production methods had to be drastically redesigned to become cost-competitive. In the pharmaceutical division, a major program in marketing and financial management was launched. Managerial thinking had to move from the assumption that R&D would always guarantee enough new drugs to enable the division to grow, to the assumption that in the future there would be very few new drugs so the emphasis had to shift to more competitive selling and tighter cost controls to protect profit margins. Most of the projects used a managed change process of the kind that was described in the previous chapter.

The task force that had the most difficult challenge was the one that had to confront the issue of lifetime employment and job security. In the chemical division and in the Basel headquarters organization, a major downsizing process had to be implemented immediately. This was accomplished by drawing heavily on *other core elements* of the culture, especially the principle of "we treat our people very well." That cultural assumption was rationalized to be even more basic than "we never lay anyone off" and enabled the downsizing to be done in a caring and humane way.

The strong paternalistic culture led to a very sensitive, carefully designed layoff process in which each person was first talked to by the boss and senior management and given a full explanation of what had to be done and why. There would be no "categories" of layoffs or pink slips delivered in the mail. Managers were trained in how to handle the personal conversations so that each person would feel that his or her case was carefully reviewed.

Supplementing this personal explanation, C-G created programs of maximizing the use of early retirements, reduction through attrition wherever possible, generous severance packages, extensive career counseling to help people find new jobs, and, most important, opportunities for transitional consulting or part-time work. One of the senior people in the human resources area was released but was given an opportunity to do a research project for six months on a consulting basis that saved his self-esteem and provided an adequate economic transition.

Some Lessons—Did Culture Change?

The core element around job security clearly changed, but I call this a "moderate" culture change because other core elements of the culture not only did not change but were, in fact, the means by which the changes were accomplished. In all of the projects, there was much talk of "culture change," but in fact C-G had enlisted its authority system, hierarchy, predilection for using groups and teams, and traditions of loyalty and subordination to make major changes in each unit and in its human relations core. In the end, C-G managers felt that they had affirmed their culture, rather than changed it, by rationalizing that they had treated people very well, even as they were making drastic changes in how they did business.

Changing business practices, reducing costs, rightsizing, and so forth, do not necessarily involve total culture change. Rather, this case illustrates the lesson that one can solve the business problems and change some dysfunctional elements of the core culture by using other core elements of the existing culture to change whatever needs changing. The same cultural dynamics are visible in the case of Alpha Power, where we can see that peripheral elements of the culture were changed without too much culture strain. Becoming environmentally responsible did not challenge the core. On the other hand, becoming a safer organization runs into a core element of the employee/union subculture—"we do not rat on our peers." Employees will tell each other how to do things safely, but they will not report unsafe practices by a fellow employee to supervisors. When part of the cultural core is a group norm held by a subculture that is integral to the performance of the organization, there is then no alternative but to create programs that involve the subculture in its own change processes toward more safety. I described some of those processes in the previous chapter, and we should recognize that safety will not reach desired levels until the union norms have changed to support employee monitoring of each other's behavior.

Drastic Culture Change in Digital Equipment Corporation

If planned and managed, culture change as described in the last chapter and in the C-G case above does not produce the business results that are needed in terms of the ideal future state, then change leaders have to seek more drastic measures. The most common of these is to bring in an outside CEO who has a different set of values and assumptions from those of the present core culture. If a hybrid manager can be found in a subculture, he or she can serve that function.

The board typically empowers the new CEO to produce a major turnaround—and explicitly or implicitly states how long he or she has to produce better business results. The extreme version of this process is to bring in a known turnaround manager who promises to bring the company back into some kind of financial health by immediately taking whatever measures are necessary, usually massive firing of senior executives, reorganizing, selling off unprofitable units, breaking the union, merging with another organization, or preparing the organization to be sold.

More measured versions of this process are exemplified by General Electric empowering Jack Welch, IBM bringing in Lou Gerstner, or Kodak selecting George Fisher. As of this writing the U.S. Congress is deciding what kind of leadership to require in the auto industry of the future in exchange for the loans that the industry is requesting. At the minimum the new "czar" of autos should be well acquainted with culture dynamics in an old and dying organization, recognizing how difficult it will be to change some of the core assumptions of the U.S. auto industry.

In the late 1980s and early 1990s, DEC faced an economic crisis of major proportions. For a variety of reasons that have been referred to throughout this book, during the 1980s DEC became slow and inefficient. Competition was stiffer, market windows were narrower, and DEC's cost structure was out of line with those of its competitors.[3] The core cultural emphasis on innovation became less relevant as computers became commodities. The managerial culture was perceived to be too egalitarian and the decision process too slow. The subunits had become too powerful and unwilling to integrate around any kind of central strategy. Ken Olsen's efforts to focus were overridden by several engineering managers who felt they understood the market better, but they were in conflict with each other on the matter of what to focus on since each had his or her own pet solution to DEC's difficulties. Conflict over strategic goals and the means to be used to achieve anything were rampant. A number of downsizing efforts were attempted, but they did not, in the board's estimation, go far enough to make DEC viable and profitable.

In late 1992 Ken Olsen resigned under pressure and the board promoted the vice president of semiconductors, Robert Palmer, to take over as CEO. The choice of Palmer to succeed Ken Olsen appeared to be motivated by bringing in someone who understood DEC, as he had spent part of his career there, but who would be much more disciplined in his approach to fixing DEC's problems. This change is an example of bringing in a hybrid manager from the subculture of semiconductors, which was built on very different assumptions, and charging him with creating a major turnaround.

If the new turnaround manager sees major barriers in the present culture, it is inevitable that a period of cultural destruction has to take place. Many managers have to evolve new ways of thinking and behaving very rapidly, or they have to be forced out of the organization and be replaced by managers who have different assumptions in the first place. In some instances (perhaps GE is a good example), a strong and charismatic leader can produce change in the existing cadre of executives. But as the case of DEC shows, the existing cadre often clings to the old culture that has made them successful and therefore has to be replaced before the business problems begin to be solved. We should have no illusions, therefore, about the possibility of major cultural transformation without massive human costs. For old cultural assumptions to be destroyed, the organization has to convert or get rid of the culture carriers.

The major changes instituted by Palmer over a period of several years were to centralize decision making, tighten discipline, shed unproductive units, and, most important, get rid of most of the carriers of the old culture. Some were fired, some retired, and many left because they could not work under the new regime. All agreed that the old DEC culture was being destroyed in favor of a more traditional autocratic and disciplined hierarchy. In their place, Palmer brought in a variety of outsiders with different experience, skills, and basic assumptions about how to run an organization. The turnaround produced a smaller and more efficient organization that was then bought by Compaq in 1998 and eventually merged into Hewlett-Packard when it acquired Compaq.

Employees who remained in DEC frequently lamented the destruction of the old culture, and many of them left to start new enterprises that would recapture the old culture. For many, the attachment to the old culture was so strong that they formed an "alumni association," created a newsletter to stay in touch with each other, and have continued to have regular reunions. Those who went to other companies attempted to institute some of the principles they felt had worked well in DEC. Paradoxically, even though the DEC culture within DEC was largely destroyed, as a set of concepts of how to run a company, that same culture survived among various ex-DEC employees.

The important point to note in this case is that the culture change could not be accomplished with the present set of players at the senior level. They were too embedded in the old way of working since it had led to DEC's success in the first place. To institute a new way of working, Palmer had to recruit another set of senior-management players. Whether this created a new culture or simply started DEC down a path of more transitions and changes is not clear, but it is obvious that DEC once again became economically viable enough to become an attractive target of acquisition for Compaq.

Lessons

The major lesson of the DEC experience is that you cannot change the core cultural assumptions by which an organization runs without removing the carriers of those cultural assumptions, but even then some of those assumptions will survive and resurface in other organizational contexts. Within the organizational context, culture destruction is a painful and brutal process in human terms, but it is also clear, from the degree to which ex-DEC employees have held on to the cultural values that they grew up with, that "the culture" was not destroyed in the heads of the people—only in the DEC organization as such.

A second lesson comes from observations of failed turnarounds. The new outside leader must become familiar enough with the old culture to understand just what needs to be changed and what kind of resistance will be encountered. The hybrids as outsiders are in a much better position to figure this out. As I mentioned in the case of Jones Food (Chapter Seven), when severe crises followed the founder's death and his lieutenant's retirement, the company attempted to bring in strong outsiders; but the existing culture of this family firm was so strong that the first three failed. Only when the family brought in a person who had been in Jones Food before and who was recruited back after a period of independent success did they find someone who could manage the necessary culture change.

The story of Apple is somewhat similar in that John Sculley and then Gilbert Amelio were evidently not able to bring about some of the changes the company needed, so the board went back to Steve Jobs—who clearly understood the culture, having been one of its founders and architects. Jobs's success in evolving Apple reflects several cultural themes. First, he went back to what was his first idea for products—"toys for Yuppies"—and extended the product concept to a broader population. Second, he clearly learned important business and managerial lessons outside of Apple in his other ventures, which he could then bring back to Apple to invigorate it.

Welch's success in GE is undoubtedly related to his having grown up in the company, and Gerstner's success in IBM is probably related to the fact that he was bringing back some of the marketing values that had so badly eroded with IBM's growth. Although these cases are often perceived as turnarounds and major culture *changes*, they are, in fact, more like destruction of a few dysfunctional core elements and *revitalizations* of other cultural elements that had been eroded and were now needed for the organization to survive.[4] The level of transformation in turnarounds of this kind has an organizational and financial logic all its own. It is unlikely that one can influence the dynamic very much from the point of view of planned change. If your organization finds itself in enough trouble to seek outside leadership, you must plan for a period of painful human dislocation.

In reviewing the various cases described in this book, it should be clear that only DEC really represents a case of destruction of the cultural core within the organization, and even then the assumptions lived on in ex-DEC members. In all the other cases, some cultural destruction took place but other core assumptions survived and were, in fact, the engine that motivated the changes that were made. Strong cultures die hard, if they die at all.

Change Leaders and Change Agents

The last several chapters have focused on evolution, learning, and transformational processes in organizations with special focus on issues of culture and subculture. In most organizational situations today, the pace of change is such that one cannot count on evolution to solve an organization's problems. Change leadership and change management are needed whether we are talking about a start-up, mid-life, or mature/dying organization. What will be required of these people?

Change leaders can be thought of as persons who create enough disconfirmation in the organization to arouse motivation to change and who can then organize the processes needed to make the changes. Both things are needed, but they need not be in the same person. Change *leadership* should therefore have several characteristics if it is to arouse motivation to change and learn:

1. Credibility. Whatever they say must be believed (not discounted).

2. Clarity of vision. Whatever they say must be clear and make sense.

3. Ability to articulate the vision. They must be able to state verbally and in writing what it is they perceive and what the implications are for the future of the organization. They must be able to translate their vision into desired new *behavior*.

4. Understanding of cultural dynamics at different stages of organizational growth.

5. Process skills to create the management processes needed to implement planned change programs that are appropriate to the organization's age, size, and business/technological/cultural context.

Once motivation is present, change *agents* (what I called earlier the "change team") can proceed with developing various processes to make it happen. Points 4 and 5 above are especially important for change agents because the actual change process to be used must be congruent with the internal and external situation that the organization finds itself in. Too many change programs treat all organizational issues as the same, but we know that culture, like personality, has unique characteristics that must be taken into account if growth and learning are to take place. Just as the therapist has to work with the unique aspects of the client's personality, so do the change leader and agent have to work with the unique aspects of organizational cultures and subcultures.

Change agents may or may not be the same persons as the change leaders. They do not need to be in positions of formal leadership; in fact, they often work more effectively as catalysts and facilitators rather than overtly as leaders (if there is already some source of motivation present). Their most important role is to implement the various steps described in the Figure 8.1 Map.

Change leaders can articulate new directions, new values, and new visions, but it is usually the change team, functioning as a temporary parallel system, that defines exactly what is required of the organization in terms of new thinking and behavior. The change team, then, must be able to function as process consultants, simultaneously diagnosing and intervening as they work through the stages of change.[5]

The Bottom Line and Change Dynamics Summary

At this point I want to review some of the main insights that have come out of the last four chapters. First, we reviewed in Chapter Six the psychological and social dynamics involved in any change process that requires unlearning as well as new learning. The change process always begins with some discon-firmation, some recognition on the part of leaders that some-thing is not working—what I have labeled *survival anxiety*. As they identify the business problem, they develop a vision of the future—the new thing to be learned. The desired new learn-ing has to be articulated in clear behavioral terms, and it is this articulation that produces resistance to change and defen-sive denial—what I have labeled *learning anxiety*. The key is to understand that resistance to change is to be expected as a nor-mal phenomenon, and that new learning will only take place if the learner is made to feel psychologically secure.

In terms of a principle for transformative change, motivation to learn the desired new behavior will only be present if survival anxiety is greater than learning anxiety; but a second principle is that the preferred way to achieve this state is to *reduce learning anxiety* by providing the learner *psychological safety*. In examin-ing all the conditions needed to create psychological safety, it becomes clear why transformative change is difficult and time-consuming. Furthermore, if *core* elements of the culture need to be transformed, planned change processes may not work, lead-ing change leaders to institute more drastic processes such as described in this chapter.

Second, we reviewed how in a planned change process a change team must become a temporary parallel system that man-ages the entire change process in terms of the stages identified in Figure 8.1. I emphasize that the change goal—the new way of thinking and behaving—must be specified quite concretely in order to determine how the present culture will aid or hin-der the change process. The more one can use the culture as an aid, the easier it is to achieve the change. If cultural elements are found to be hindrances, then new change processes have to be designed to deal with them. Sometimes those processes are the drastic ones such as described in this chapter, but one should not automatically assume that every change is a culture change.

If basic assumptions are really to be changed without destroying and rebuilding the organization, transformations require anywhere from five to fifteen years or more. It takes time to construct the parallel system, learn new assumptions, and then design processes that allow the assumptions to be introduced into the original organization. Recall the Procter & Gamble example from Chapter One; it took fifteen years for all of the plants to convert to the new manufacturing system.

If you are the change agent, try not to short-circuit the above steps. The temptation to launch into immediate action and announce a "culture change program" is tremendous, but where culture is involved it is better to go slow initially and make sure you have figured out what the new way of thinking and working is, and how the culture can aid or hinder you before you launch major new initiatives. It is especially important to figure out how the culture can aid you—how you can build on the present culture to accomplish the needed changes.

Part Three

THE REALITIES OF MULTICULTURALISM

The final two chapters deal with the realities of how the world is changing through the impacts of information technology, the growing complexity of all the fields of business and organization leading to the formation of subcultures nested in larger cultures, and the globalism that is forcing cultures and subcultures into new kinds of multicultural interactions. Chapter Ten focuses on some of the issues of cultural interaction and Chapter Eleven both reviews and looks forward to the emerging realities for future leaders of a multicultural world.

10

WHEN CULTURES MEET

Acquisitions, Mergers, Joint Ventures, and Other Multicultural Collaborations

The Multi-Culture Problem

Cultures meet any time there is a merger of two companies, when one company acquires another, when two companies engage in a joint venture, or when a new group is created with members from several cultures. A merger attempts to blend two cultures, without necessarily treating one or the other as dominant. In an acquisition, the acquired organization automatically becomes a subculture in the larger culture of the acquiring company. In the joint venture the new organization must start with bringing two cultures together from scratch. And in the new group situation, individuals from several cultures have to figure out how to work together without any one culture being the dominant one.

All of these situations are fundamentally different from anything we have talked about so far because they may involve the *simultaneous* meeting of national, occupational, and organizational cultures. Each culture is, from the point of view of its members, the correct way to perceive, feel about, and act on daily events. Each culture may have opinions and biases about "the other," but by definition our own culture is always the one that is "right." Getting cross-cultural organizations, projects, joint ventures, and teams to work together therefore poses a much larger cultural challenge than the change problems we have discussed in the last chapters, where mostly organizational cultures and subcultures were involved.

An extreme version of this problem is well illustrated in the medical organizations that deal with immigrants from cultures that have different norms and values about how to deal with medical problems. Not only is there a language problem in giving instructions about prescriptions, but the patient may believe that the medicines will be harmful and secretly not take them.[1] The business version of this dilemma occurred in a Canadian-Italian joint venture in which various memos with important instructions from the Canadian parent were systematically ignored by the Italians in the venture because they believed that anything of importance should and would be *personally* communicated. The memos were viewed as insulting and rationalized as being unimportant.

Variations in occupational cultures can breed the same kinds of problems, as was the case in Ciba-Geigy when headquarters attempted to create a management development program to improve marketing skills. The program was offered to the chemical, agricultural, and pharmaceutical managers, but when it was discovered that they would be taking the program *together*, they balked on the grounds that marketing was "far too different in each of these sectors." How could people who sold drugs to doctors have anything in common with salesmen who slogged around in muddy fields selling new kinds of fertilizer to farmers? Clearly the designers felt that there were general marketing principles that everyone could and should learn, but it was very difficult to convince the different occupational groups that such was the case.

A further problem in these multicultural enterprises is that culture is typically not considered in their initial formation. Whether we are talking about mergers, acquisitions, joint ventures, or temporary partnerships and task forces, economic, strategic, and political considerations dominate the decision whether to go ahead or not. It is assumed that the cultural issues can be solved later once the new unit has been created. Even when culture is considered as part of the due diligence process prior to consummation of the deal, it is rarely given a central role, in spite of the fact that the failure of such enterprises is often attributed after the fact to cultural mismatches.

In the case of mergers, the problem of separation, domination, blending, or conflict is compounded by the fact that the new unit does not have any shared history, so one or the other subunit probably feels inferior, threatened, angry, and defensive.[2] In most of these situations, we are dealing with the interaction of two or possibly three cultures that have to accommodate to each other over a period of time.

A whole new set of intercultural issues arises in the various kinds of temporary or ad hoc organizations that are increasingly being created in today's global environment. This point is best illustrated by what is being called "collaborations," such as a United Nations health team consisting of members from several countries operating together in yet another country, or an engineering team from a global service company such as Schlumberger being sent to another country to help with oil production.

"Participants in a collaboration may come together on a one-time basis, without anticipating continued interaction. A core set of members may remain involved for an extended period of time, but other participants may float on and off the effort, working only on an 'as needed' sporadic basis. Further, collaborations may have periods of intensely interdependent interaction, but may otherwise consist of quite independent actors. Many are not embedded in a single organizational context, but represent either cross-organizational cooperation, or participants may not have any organizational affiliation at all. Participants may feel as though they share a common purpose for the duration of a given project, yet may not view themselves as a 'team.' Collaborators may never meet face-to-face, may be geographically dispersed, and may be primarily connected by communication technology. Thus collaborations are more loosely structured, more temporary, more fluid, and often more electronically enabled than traditional teams."[3]

The cultural issue is fundamentally different in most of these situations because the work group itself is already multicultural, both in terms of nationality and occupational background. In the previous analysis we have dealt with members of subcultures launching change processes that impacted members of other subcultures and, thereby, changed elements of the total corporate culture. In these situations, any given department, project, task force, or standing committee may already consist of members from two or more different national and corporate cultures, leading from the outset to potential difficulties in communication, decision making, and performance.

A further complexity is provided by the growing number of teams, task forces, and other kinds of collaborations that are not co-located. For example, a number of consulting companies are abandoning the McKinsey model of hiring a broad range of experts to put into project teams. Instead, they are hiring a large pool of individual experts on virtually everything that a client might need help with and then putting together teams that might or might not work in physical proximity. The question of how cultural issues will manifest themselves in these kinds of collaborations remains to be seen.

To deal with these broader multicultural issues, we will first review what I have already said about merger, acquisition, and joint venture issues where organizational as well or national cultures are involved and then examine the issues of multicultural units such as "collaborations" later in the chapter.

The Role of Cultural Assessment in Mergers, Acquisitions, and Joint Ventures

The merger, acquisition, or joint venture agenda is usually driven by the more overt characteristics of organizations, such as shared or compatible technologies, shared business goals, financial compatibility, common markets, and product synergy. Often overlooked until too late is that the *means* by which the goals are accomplished in the two organizations may be very different, and the underlying *assumptions* about business and human processes may actually conflict with one another. Rarely checked are those aspects that might be considered "cultural": the philosophy or style of the company; technological origins, which might provide clues as to basic assumptions; beliefs about its mission and future; and how it organizes itself internally. Yet a cultural mismatch in an acquisition, merger, or joint venture is as great a risk as a financial, product, or market mismatch.

Some concrete examples will make this point clear. Some years ago, General Foods (GF) purchased Burger Chef, a successful chain of hamburger restaurants. But despite ten years of concerted effort, the parent could not make the acquisition profitable. First, GF did not anticipate that many of the best Burger Chef managers would leave because they did not like GF's management philosophy. Then, instead of hiring new managers with experience in the fast-food business, GF assigned some of its own managers to run the new business. This was its second mistake, since these managers did not understand the technology and operations of the fast-food business. Their efforts to use many of the marketing techniques that had proved to be effective in the manufactured food business proved to be useless. Third, GF imposed on Burger Chef many of the control systems and procedures that had historically proved useful for GF, not realizing that this would drive the operating costs of the chain too high. GF's managers never completely understood franchise operations and hence could not get a feel for what it would take to run that kind of business profitably. Eventually GF sold Burger Chef, having lost many millions of dollars over a decade. With hindsight, it was clear that GF never understood that a fast-food business creates a very different kind of culture than a manufacturing package-food business does.

Lack of understanding of the cultural risks of buying a franchised business was brought out even more clearly in another case. United Fruit, at the time a stuffy, traditional, moralistic company whose management prided itself on high ethical standards, bought a chain of fast-food restaurants that were locally franchised all around the country. The company's managers discovered, much to their chagrin, that one of the biggest of these restaurants and its associated motel was the local brothel. The activities of the town were so well integrated around this restaurant/motel that the alternative of closing it down posed the risk of drawing precisely the kind of attention United Fruit wanted at all costs to avoid. The managers asked themselves, after the fact, "Should we have known what our acquisition involved on this not-very-obvious level? Should we have understood our own value system better, to ensure compatibility?" So a great deal of effort had to be expended to keep this acquisition functioning while hiding potentially embarrassing information.

A third example highlighting the clash of two sets of assumptions about authority is the case of the two first-generation high-tech companies. Company A, run by a founder who injected strong beliefs that one succeeds by stimulating initiative and egalitarianism, was bought by Company B, this one run by a strongly autocratic entrepreneur who trained his employees to be highly disciplined and formal. The purchasing company (B) wanted and needed the acquiree's managerial talent, but within one year of the deal most of the best managers from Company A had left because they could not adapt to the formal autocratic style of Company B. The autocratic entrepreneur could not understand why this happened and had no sensitivity to the cultural differences between the two companies.

What is striking in these cases is the lack of insight on the part of the acquiring company into its own organizational culture, its unconscious assumptions about how a business should be run. Contemplating some recent major mergers (such as Citicorp and Travelers, AMOCO and British Petroleum, Chrysler and Daimler Benz), one can only wonder how these corporate giants will mesh not only their businesses but also their cultures. The histories of these companies suggest that substantial cultural differences almost certainly exist between them.

So would it not have been helpful to do mutual cultural assessments before the deals were consummated? Paradoxically, there are several reasons why this would not be useful or even possible. One reason is that prior to the merger the negotiations leading up to it often have to be kept secret. Each organization could do a *self*-assessment but would not have the license or ability to get into the other organization to find out how it really works. A more important second reason why culture assessment before a merger would not be useful is the general point I have been making that you would not know what to assess. Until organizations are actually meshed, they usually don't discover where the cultures conflict. Until Ciba-Geigy acquired Airwick, it had no way of knowing that its own culture was so strongly built around scientific breakthroughs and solving the world's important food and health problems.

However, once a merger is publicly announced, it would make complete sense to engage in such formal assessment. The two organizations could form a series of task forces with equal numbers of participants from each cultural unit. These task forces could then assess the artifacts, espoused values, and shared tacit assumptions in the main areas of mission, goals, means, measurement, corrective mechanisms, language, group boundaries, and status and reward systems. The work of such "integration units" is typically done in one of two ways: (1) examine each business process to determine how to take the best elements of each merging or joint venture organization, leading to some blend of the different cultures or (2) examine each business process, decide immediately which organization's process is best suited to the future enterprise, and impose that process on the new joint unit.

For example, I was told by an ex-DEC manager who was part of the integration team that planned the merger of HP with

Compaq that they decided from the outset it would take too long and be too anxiety-provoking to try to blend the old DEC, the old Compaq, and the old HP ways. Instead, they opted to examine each process, make a decision immediately as to which one was best suited for the future, and simply imposed it on the new merged organization.

In the case of outright *acquisitions* the parent company will, of course, impose some of its core processes immediately, even when this is dysfunctional. Recall that the Ciba-Geigy chief financial officer told Airwick Europe they would not be allowed to develop their own streamlined accounting system because the parent company's system was "adequate." In that case it made life difficult for Airwick to function optimally. In another case of GE acquiring the Italian company Nuovo Pignone, not only did GE impose its financial and accounting system on the Italian organization but they combined it with intensive skill training to get across the knowledge and values that lay behind it, thus launching a much more intense process of imposing the GE culture around leadership, accountability, and performance measurement.[4] This and similar cases have been used to make the argument that the imposition of the accounting and performance measurement system is, in fact, the best initial step in forcing more general cultural blending. By starting with the business process that is most fundamental to the health of the organization, its financial system, the acquiring organization can claim legitimacy for its imposition. It was observed in Nuovo Pignone that the initial resistance to the broader elements of the GE culture was gradually overcome as the Italians noted that the GE financial process was successful. This eventually led to the adoption of other GE values and a real set of evolutionary changes in the old Nuovo Pignone culture.

The *joint ventures* that are springing up all over the globe involve not only different *corporate* cultures but even different *national* cultures. When two sets of cultures meet, the basic problem is that more than one culture must be aligned, reconciled, merged, or absorbed. Would it not be advisable for each parent company to educate the members of the future joint venture in the cultural essentials of the other culture or cultures involved? Paradoxically the answer is not clear. On the one hand, it would seem to be essential to learn the language and customs of the other culture in order to communicate and avoid being offensive by breaking basic rules. On the other hand, it builds stereotypes of the other culture that can get in the way of joint learning.

For example, in a U.S.-German joint venture, each parent decided to provide cross-cultural training on what the other culture was like, and the venture budgeted for a one-week outward-bound-type experience to help the two teams to come together. The initial company training created strong stereotypes, and unfortunately the joint training was canceled for reasons of time and money. The early work interactions were therefore heavily dominated by the learned stereotypes.[5] This showed up, for example, in trying to set production targets; the Germans assumed that the U.S. numbers were always inflated since "Americans always expect budgets and targets to be cut by higher management." On the other hand, the Americans were warned that "Germans are always too conservative in their projections." Each side tried to give fairly accurate numbers but totally mistrusted the numbers from the other group, making it difficult to reach a realistic budget figure. Neither group was able to bring this out into the open lest they offend each other. So each group would complain to the researcher but argue that things could not be brought up in meetings.

Some cultural blending eventually resulted from a business crisis. Production was well below what either group had predicted, there were unanticipated labor problems, and the U.S. parent changed key managers after these problems arose. To fix the problems, the two nationalities finally got together as a single group and chose procedures on the basis of which cultural assumptions were best suited to solving the new external problem. In the labor relations area, the Germans ended up leaning more on the Americans, but in the technical area the reverse happened; gradually, a new way of working was forged by taking some assumptions from each parent.

We can speculate in cases like these whether or not an outward-bound type of program that forces joint interaction in a non-work setting would have been helpful. Such programs would surely improve informal communication, but it is not clear whether or not the stereotypes would have been overcome once back at work.

In summary, self-assessment and assessment of the other culture is not an automatic solution to cross-cultural effectiveness. Learning each other's languages or adopting a common language is certainly essential, but beyond that it may well be that the essential cross-cultural learning is accomplished best in the work setting, where common work problems can guide the learning process. Once again, the point is that cultural analysis works best in the context of a shared problem. Or, as the Russian manager of HR in the joint venture of British Petroleum and its Russian counterpart responded when asked how she could help these two very different organizations come together: "Forced interaction."

New Issues in Collaborations and Other Multicultural Organizations

The problems that arise in joint ventures become even more salient in the new forms of multicultural organizations that have been called "collaborations." When the group working together contains members from three or more cultures and may be operating in yet a fourth different culture, or may not be co-located at all, what kinds of cultural issues are likely to come up? For example, in a large Brazilian chemical company that had been formed by a merger of a Brazilian unit with German and French units, the following embarrassing situation arose. The merger agreement had provided for the chairmanship of the Brazilian company to rotate among the partners, from the original national units and it was now the turn of the former head of the German unit to take over the board. He developed a very careful agenda, organized it thoroughly with time allocations to different items, and confidently presented it at the first board meeting to get things going. The detailed written agenda was circulated and when the chair opened the meeting by going to the first item, the Brazilians in the group burst out in laughter. Not only did they regard this degree of organization ridiculous but they also demonstrated by their laughter a culturally different attitude toward authority. The German chair not only had to deal with his embarrassment at being laughed at but with his ignorance of the norms that evidently had developed in this multicultural board, which was based heavily on the Brazilian culture of informality.

Misunderstanding the rules and norms surrounding the issue of authority is probably the most common problem in newly formed multicultural groups. The high degree of formality that is associated with diplomacy can be understood as a defense against making mistakes in this cultural arena. But formality itself can lead to problems if there is insufficient understanding. For example, in a formal classroom setting, I observed the following variations in response to the same lecture material if I asked "Are there any questions or comments?" In the United States, American managers were quick to raise their hands and invariably asked questions about how the content that had been discusses would be *useful*. The same material taught in the United Kingdom elicited from British managers a spirited theoretical discussion of the material with the wonderfully masked disagreement that would always be preceded by "but one would have thought. . . ." The French and Italians always zeroed in on the details and got especially involved if they perceived some logical inconsistency in what had been presented. The Asian students, even managers, typically did not raise their hands at all for one of two reasons. In China there was a norm of deference to the professor that inhibited individuals from raising questions, but I learned that if I gave them a chance to discuss the material among themselves for a few minutes they could then raise questions through one of their representatives. With Japanese managers I discovered that they were very conscious of their status hierarchy and it was not appropriate to speak before one of the higher-status persons had spoken.

In the work situation, if the leader is from a culture in which it is expected that subordinates will speak up if they have a relevant piece of information, but he or she is dealing with group members whose norms dictate that one does not speak up until the boss specifically asks, and even then one suppresses information that would embarrass the boss, one can foresee that this group will have difficulty being effective. Misunderstandings around authority then have a direct impact on the quality of communication that is possible.

Lest we think that this is only a problem across national boundaries, consider the problems caused by different norms around these issues in occupational communities. The engineering culture had clearly defined the problem of the unsafe O-rings under cold weather conditions in the flight of the Challenger and had made an effort to communicate their concern but were overridden by the norms of the managerial culture in which cost, schedule, and political commitments overrode the data.[6]

The multicultural problem, then, is how to create a group situation that enables sufficient task-relevant communication to occur so that the group can perform its essential function. Is the solution better initial selection, cultural training prior to creating the group, a leadership style that encourages openness, joint training once the group has been formed, training in Dialogue, or all of the above?

Initial Selection

Is there such a thing as "cultural intelligence" that can be tested for so that only people with high scores are put into multicultural team situations and collaborations? Some scholars have developed and validated a self-administering scale that measures self-perceived desire to know other cultures and willingness to develop skills in dealing with other cultures.[7] This would be a useful tool if one had enough candidates for the jobs and if it was appropriate to use a test. For example, this might not be appropriate in the selection of a senior executive. Another basis for selection could be actual cross-cultural experience. In a study of senior executives in Ciba-Geigy, we had found that international assignments that led to cross-cultural experience were a good predictor of promotion and effective performance at more senior levels where cross-cultural issues were more pressing.

A more subtle but possibly more relevant way to locate culturally "intelligent" people is to observe how they behave in situations that involve different occupational cultures. For example, in product development teams that include members from marketing, manufacturing, and engineering, how ready are members to try to understand each other's points of view?[8] You might discover that the engineer who is interested in and willing to listen to the marketer would also be interested in and willing to listen to someone from another national culture.

Occupational cultures produce inter-cultural problems of the same sort that national cultures do, so sensitivity to others with different assumptions and values can be observed meaningfully within organizations. Sensitivity to interpersonal and group processes is probably the most important dimension to observe. The German manager in the Brazilian company clearly had very little sensitivity to how groups work, poor observation skills, and possibly very little desire to work with other cultures.

Providing Knowledge and Training

Much research has been done on how countries and their cultures differ, especially by Hofstede in his massive multicultural survey of all the units of IBM.[9] Many books have been written and training programs developed to educate and train managers and employees who are about to be sent to another culture in the norms of that culture. This approach suggests that *knowledge* of other cultures would ameliorate communication breakdowns and ineffective collaborations. However, this approach suffers from the same problem that culture assessments inside organizations do, as was argued earlier in this chapter. Until there is a problem focus, the information about another culture is not only vast but lacks focus. Knowing that the Brazilians tend to be informal and more egalitarian would not have prevented the German manager from approaching the group the way he did. On the other hand, if the board had decided to examine its own working style, then it would have been revealed that the Brazilian managers had little patience for formality.

An even bigger problem is that prior training on other cultures can lead to inappropriate stereotyping and perceptual biases. Knowing what the Japanese in general are like and value does not guarantee that the particular Japanese who is in your newly constituted task force will behave in that way. Furthermore, if he or she does behave that way and validates the stereotype, this insight does little to facilitate better communication. It only avoids offending the other. Certainly it is important to know what kinds of things will be offensive in other cultures, but that will not be enough to build good working relationships.

Leadership Style and Attitude

Leadership of the multicultural unit is crucial along two dimensions: (1) the leader must stimulate open communication around the tasks to be performed and (2) the leader must create a climate in which his or her authority is NOT a barrier to communication. It has to be OK to tell the boss things, even things that the boss is doing wrong. Here again some of the best examples come not from cross-national but from cross-occupational groups. For example, when a new procedure was introduced into cardiac surgery that required tighter coordination between the surgeon, the anesthesiologist, the perfusionist who monitored the heart-lung by-pass machine, and the nurses, it was found that successful adoption of this less-invasive method depended very much on the initial attitude of the surgeon as leader of the group.[10] The most successful groups were created by leaders who acknowledged the interdependency, reduced status differences by joining the rest of the team in joint training, and encouraged *mutual* coaching as different members of the team observed ways that some of their behavior could be made more effective.

Because the leader is in a position of authority, it is the leader who is most likely to cut off communication unwittingly, especially with cultural groups where upward communication is difficult in the first place. Just as it is difficult for a Japanese manager to talk back to a U.S. professor, so it is hard for a nurse or a technician to talk back to a senior surgeon. *It is up to the person in the leadership position to create the climate and conditions for such communication to occur, and to coach the members of the team by encouraging and rewarding feedback and analysis.*

Creating a climate of open communications sometimes requires special events in which status boundaries are deliberately blurred. For example, in the very formal Ciba-Geigy, at each annual three-day meeting of senior executives one afternoon was always devoted to everyone playing at some sport that would reduce everyone to the same level of incompetence, for example, shooting crossbows or hitting a ball with a club head that was attached to a two-foot leather thong at the end of a three-foot rigid club. Following this common humiliation, we all went to an informal dinner at which everyone was randomly seated to mix up the various ranks represented. Conversation flowed freely and one could see that subordinates found ways in this setting to get messages across to their superiors. The Japanese ritual of going out drinking with the boss so that things can be said under the influence that could never be said at the workplace has a similar function.

Joint Training Prior to and on the Job

The surgical teams that learned successfully how to do the new procedure all underwent joint training, while the ones who found it too difficult were "ad hoc" teams of experts in their specialties but had no joint experience. It was the attitude of the leader that led to the joint training in the first place, but it was the actual shared experience that allowed the members of the different occupational cultures to get to know each other and to develop reliable communication processes. In a multi-national team, such joint training would be even more relevant because both national and occupational culture differences would have to be dealt with.

Regular Process Reviews

Once on the job, multicultural groups need to build into their working routines some process reviews, post-mortems, and other mechanisms to jointly review and analyze their work and their process. Again it is the leader who must call for this and set the tone so that people will feel free to say what they observed and what they felt about it, even if that means giving feedback to the more high-status members and the leaders. Different cultural styles will then reveal themselves but also be subject to group analysis and the setting of new norms if needed.

In spite of all the mechanisms I have described so far, the danger remains that members of such groups will develop too rapidly the illusion that they now understand each other. To deal with that danger, a more powerful approach is needed to enable mutual understanding across cultural boundaries.

Culture Traps (the Illusion That We Understand One Another)

All of the kinds of inter-cultural situations I have described so far have in common the problem of how to establish valid communication across an occupational or national culture boundary. I have singled this out for special attention because the most dangerous trap in cross-cultural communication is the *illusion* that we understand each other. If we speak different languages, we know that we do not understand and accept the need for an interpreter. But if the organization or group uses a common language such as English, the potential for misunderstanding is great.

A recent example illustrates the issue. I received an e-mail telling me that one of my books was being translated into Chinese and would I be willing to provide a short preface for this translation. I agreed, wrote the preface, and sent it off. The Chinese publisher sent back a further request for a photograph to put in the book and for an autograph. I sent the photo but was reluctant to send an autograph, both for security reasons and because I did not see how this could be accomplished with e-mail. I did, however, suggest that if they had a fax number, maybe I could get the autograph to them that way. They sent me a fax number, I faxed the signature, but got a further e-mail saying that they had not received it. At this point, out of patience, I sent an e-mail saying that they should just list my name and affiliation, that they did not need a signature. They wrote back thanking me for providing exactly what they needed. Evidently what they meant by "autograph" was just how I wanted my name and affiliation to be printed at the end of the preface. My literal translation caused a lot of unnecessary work and irritation.

Research on product development teams showed how a similar kind of issue can arise around occupational cultures.[11] The teams agreed that their effectiveness would be a function of maximizing the amount of "*information* about customers" that they had. They felt satisfied that they had enough information to proceed with product development, but it turned out that the engineers defined information as "knowledge of what customers needed in the way of technical solutions," the manufacturing members of the team defined information as "knowing how customers used equipment," marketing members defined information as "how many customers are out there," and planning members defined information as "what would they pay for the equipment." Until the group sorted this out and realized how differently they were defining the simple word "information," they could not really develop products that would meet customer demands.

When mergers, acquisitions, joint ventures, and collaborations are designed it is often on the basis of how well the externals such as products and markets fit, and the assumption is made that people of goodwill will figure each other out and make the necessary accommodations to work together. To show goodwill, we also tend to exaggerate the degree to which we actually do understand each other.

In the cross-cultural setting, one reason we exaggerate the degree of mutual understanding is to avoid the pain of being "unknown." If I am asked to work with someone from another organization and he or she has never worked with me, it is painful to realize that I have to establish my identity from scratch. It is less painful to assume that we are probably basically alike and proceed from there. Only later might we suddenly discover great differences in how we operate or that words we were using meant different things to each other.

At that point, a second trap is usually sprung: the need to cling to and justify my own way of doing things. Suddenly my way seems to make complete sense and I cannot for the life of me figure out why the "other" wants to do things differently. I am likely at this point to go into a persuasion mode and to stereotype others as not making sense if they don't agree with me.

This springs the third trap in cross-cultural communication: our disagreement and our stereotype are themselves undiscussable. We have no way of backing off and examining our assumptions without risking offending the other person or demeaning ourselves. Instead, we maintain a pretence of understanding each other and make compromises on effectiveness. To get past these traps we need to create settings in which new communication norms can be developed so that discussing misunderstanding does not become a threat to each other's "face." Such new norms can only be built with efforts at *dialogue*.[12]

The Need for Dialogue at Cultural Boundaries

If we take culture seriously, we will realize that two or more cultures trying to meet and work together constructively have to go beyond the kind of culture assessment I have described because they do not know whether they are even using the same meanings for seemingly shared concepts. To reap cultural insights at this level either as total organizations or as members of collaborations requires either participating in each other's cultures by actually sending employees into the other group for some period of time, or creating dialogues between members of the cultures that allow differing assumptions and meanings to surface. How does one create such dialogues?

The Dialogue Process

Dialogue is a form of conversation that allows the participants to relax sufficiently to begin examining the assumptions that lie behind their thought processes. Instead of trying to solve problems rapidly, the dialogue process attempts to slow down the conversation to allow participants to reflect on what comes out of their own mouths and what they hear from the mouths of others. The key to initiating dialogic conversation is to create a setting in which participants feel secure enough to suspend their need to win arguments, clarify everything they say, and challenge each other every time they disagree. In a Dialogue, if someone has just said something that I disagree with, suspension would mean that I would hold back voicing my disagreement and, instead, silently ask myself why I disagree and what assumptions I am making that might explain the disagreement.

Dialogue is more a low-key "talking around the campfire," allowing enough time for and encouraging reflective conversation, rather than confrontational conversation, discussion, or debate. But its purpose is not just to have a quiet, reflective conversation; rather, it is to allow participants to begin to see where their deeper levels of thought and tacit assumptions differ. Paradoxically, such reflection leads to better listening in that, if I identify my own assumptions and filters first, I am less likely to mishear or misunderstand the subtle meanings in the words of others. I cannot understand another culture if I have no insight into my own.

For this to work, all of the parties to the dialogue have to be willing to suspend impulses to disagree, challenge, clarify, and elaborate. By slowing down the conversation, we learn to hear the deeper layers of our own discourse and realize how much our perceptions, thoughts, and feelings are based on learned assumptions. We begin to experience our own culture, that is, the degree to which our own group identifications and backgrounds color our thought processes. As we discover this in ourselves, we are more ready to hear it and accept it in others.

Using Dialogue as the conversational process requires the imposition of certain rules such as not interrupting, talking to the symbolic campfire instead of to each other, limiting eye contact, and, most important of all, starting with a "check-in." Checking in at the beginning of the meeting means that each member in turn will say something to the group as a whole, the campfire, about his or her present mental state, motivation, or feelings. Only when all of the members have checked in is the group ready for a more free-flowing conversation. The check-in ensures that everyone has made an initial contribution to the group and stimulates some reflection rather than assertion.

An example of discovering our own culture typically arises around the instruction to talk to the campfire and avoid eye contact. For some people this is very easy, but for others, for example, American human resource professionals, this is very difficult because in U.S. culture looking at each other is considered "good communication," and this is reinforced by the professional norms in the human resource field that eye contact is necessary to make the other feel that you are really listening. We also discover that culturally Americans are made uncomfortable by periods of silence, leading them to speak up to try to move the group, while members of some other cultures find the silence comforting and an opportunity to think and observe. In both of these examples, the important discovery is not how the *other* feels but that our own assumptions about eye contact and need to fill silence by activity is itself *culturally* determined, not some absolute principle. Once I realize how many of my biases are cultural, I can hear more clearly the biases of others.

In another kind of example, the need for dialogue in a cross-*occupational* context arose when members of the Exploration and Production Division of a large oil company were asked by senior management to review how they were measured now and should be measured in the future. After many hours of making lists and debating, the group discovered that they really were two very different subcultures—an exploration culture that was built around a trial-and-error process that produced mostly failures but occasional big wins, while the production culture was built around the need for absolute reliability so that every well that was discovered could be reliably and safely exploited.

I suggested a Dialogue session in which we would take three or so hours just to explore the semantics of the word "measurement," with emphasis on all of the emotional connotations that this word had in the two subcultures. We started with an elaborated check-in by asking each member, without interruption and in turn, to talk out what the word measurement meant to him or her. Not only did this reveal the depth of the difference between the occupational subcultures of exploration and production, but it clarified to senior management that they would have to use different measurement criteria for the two groups. For exploration they needed big rewards for occasional rare events, and for production they needed immediate rewards for reliable performance and the *avoidance* of rare events (explosions, etc.).

Most of the mechanisms for stimulating cross-cultural understanding such as joint training, process reviews, after-action reviews, and Dialogue are not usually part of the daily routines of organizational life. They have to be designed as "cultural islands" and added to the normal flow of work.

The Bottom Line

Organizations, task forces, committees, and other collaborations that consist of members from several occupational and/or national cultures have a major problem of developing reliable communication. Even if they speak the same basic language, it is likely that different meanings to common words, different standards of judgment, and different assumptions about when and how one should communicate across authority and status lines will hamper effective job performance.

The kinds of assessment process referred to in relation to organizational cultures and subcultures—that is, just comparing artifacts and espoused values around various business processes—does not reveal enough about the shared, tacit, underlying assumptions, although such comparison of artifacts can be a good start for a cross-cultural dialogue.

Once the new organization is about to be formed, if cultural understanding is to arise it is essential to create Dialogue groups to explore each other's shared assumptions. Only by creating reflective dialogues is there a chance to overcome inevitable defensiveness and the illusion of similarity. After joint operations begin, a new culture is gradually built as the resulting organization together faces new tasks and learns how to deal with them. To speed up cultural learning, you should create such joint tasks early in the life of the new group.

The leaders of such groups must, at the outset, be aware of the cultural traps and minimize their operation through selection of culturally sensitive members, joint training that includes periods of Dialogue, opportunities for review and analysis of work accomplished leading to further periods of Dialogue, and perpetual display through their own behavior of commitment to open, task-relevant communication. Such norms of openness do not require members to get into personal or interpersonal issues, but leaders must emphasize that information relevant to task performance must travel freely across hierarchical and cultural boundaries if multicultural groups are to be effective.

If a joint venture, partnership, merger, or acquisition is at the stage at which the participants can be revealed to each other and to the public, the planners should then create focused Dialogues around the major elements of the strategy, goals, and means to be used in the new organization. Operationally, this means:

- Creating a series of task forces whose membership is from both cultures
- Asking the new intercultural groups to explore major areas of how each organization operates
- Training each task force to use Dialogue as the major vehicle for their conversation

How to Set Up a Dialogue

1. Select ten to twenty people who represent the cultures equally or work with the existing group (collaboration).
2. Seat everyone in a circle, or as near to it as possible.

3. Lay out the purpose of the Dialogue: "to be able to listen more reflectively to ourselves and to each other, to get a sense of the similarities and differences in our cultures."

4. Start the conversation by having the members in turn check in by introducing who they are and what goals they have for the meeting. Ask people to talk to the group as a whole (the campfire) and prohibit any questions or comments until everyone has checked in.

5. After everyone has checked in, launch a very general question, such as, "What was it like to come into this company (or into this task group)?" Everyone in the circle should, in turn, answer the question for his or her company, with the ground rule that there be no interruptions or questions until everyone has given an answer.

6. Encourage an open conversation on what everyone has just heard without the constraints of proceeding in order or having to withhold questions and comments.

7. If the topic runs dry or the group loses energy, introduce another question, for example, "How are decisions made in this organization?" Again, have everyone in turn give an answer before general conversation begins.

8. Let the differences emerge naturally; don't try to make general statements, because the purpose is mutual understanding, not necessarily clear description or conclusion.

9. After a couple of hours, ask the group to poll itself by asking each person in turn to share one or two insights about either his or her own culture or the other one; these can be written down.

10. Depending on time available, continue the process, or plan another meeting, or do the same thing with another group.

If the new organization is a multicultural group or a collaboration, the same process would be used, but the initial question

for the check-in might be something specific that would highlight cultural differences such as: "In your country (organization) what do you do when the boss asks you to do something
that you strongly disagree with?"

Again, the goal is to avoid one-on-one conversations, questions, or arguments, stimulating instead a listening climate such
that members will be less self-conscious and less worried about
self-presentation. Talking to the campfire is crucial because the
campfire does not talk back.

We have now reviewed most of the cultural issues that leaders, managers, consultants, and group members are likely to face.
How the insights gained can be used will depend very much on
the local situation you are in, but there are some realities that
cut across all of the situations, and the last chapter of this book
attempts to describe what those realities are.

Questions for the Reader

- Try to remember some occasions when you really misun-
  derstood what someone else really meant and ask yourself
  what cultural biases might have been operating to cause the
  misunderstanding. The most likely place for this to have
  happened is when you were talking with someone from
  another occupational subculture.

- Think back to how you learned to use information technology. Can you remember misunderstandings between yourself
  and your instructors?

- As you look ahead to entering another national culture, how
  will you make sure to minimize cultural misunderstanding?

11

CULTURAL REALITIES FOR THE SERIOUS CULTURE LEADER

If you are serious about managing culture in your organization, you face great danger if you do not fully appreciate the extent, depth, and power of culture in all of its manifestations. I have seen over and over again in some fifty years of consulting in this area that we look for simplification, and when someone comes along and offers us an easier way to assess and manage culture, we leap at it, only to discover later that we were dealing with surface phenomena that were not linked to real cultural forces.

Culture is deep, extensive, and stable. It cannot be taken lightly. If you do not manage culture, it will manage you—and you may not even be aware of the extent to which this is happening. But this is not easy. It is particularly annoying to managers that culture is not easily measured and controlled. In the occupational culture of management to be able to measure and control things is a sacred cow. If you can't put numbers on it, it is "soft stuff" not to be trusted or taken seriously. Cultural forces therefore pose an automatic problem because they cannot be controlled. However uncomfortable it may be, with globalism and new forms of multicultural organizations springing up all over, leaders and managers have no choice but to deal with some uncontrollable cultural realities. Of course, the leader and manager of the future will notice that the managerial occupational culture is itself evolving toward taking seriously the management of less controllable forces. People, markets, economic forces, production processes—all are becoming less predictable and less controllable by traditional methods, while information technology is opening up new ways of monitoring and "controlling."

For example, consider the growth of multicultural task forces that are working on a joint project but are not co-located. How is work assigned? How is work monitored? How is work rewarded? One organization that offers to create such projects by linking people with skills to people who need a certain kind of work done also offers the managers an automatic monitoring device built into the software to periodically check up on whether the work is being done. Note that, in this new way of thinking, the proponents glibly make the assumption that all work is done *on the computer*. How would conversations be monitored?

Perhaps most challenging of all to the new leaders will be the reality that the concept of an organization and the concept of an employee are themselves evolving in directions that will make the location of cultural issues harder to identify. For example, if the surgical team has hired a nurse from a culture in which authority is very strict, when and how will the senior surgeon discover and learn to deal with the nurse's inability and unwillingness to speak up to the surgeon when he or she observes a mistake being made?

If the team is working on a project that does not require face-to-face interaction, how will the leader find out whether communication among the team members is hampered by cultural misunderstanding or not, and what would he or she do about it if there are problems?

The solution to many of these issues is to find ways to build new cultures quickly. We know how to do this if the group can be brought together through joint forced interaction in Outward Bound and other kinds of emotionally intense experiences. One unit of Unilever has taken this to a whole new level by taking groups of young high-potential managers into remote places such as the deserts of Jordan or the riverbanks of the Li River in China.[1]

Less intense would be Dialogue groups of the sort described in the last chapter, but those only work well if the members are motivated to try to understand each other; it is not yet clear how future leaders will induce such motivation when bringing people physically together is not only expensive but may seem superfluous to some members because they have come to believe that "any group of people of good will can work together."

The upshot of this is that the leaders of the future will not know exactly what kinds of cultural issues they will encounter. They will not know whether the occupational cultures that are arising in all of the fields will be strong or weak, but if they understand cultural dynamics in general they will have diagnostic tools and approaches that will help them decipher the situations they may encounter. So a review of cultural realities is useful whether or not the issues are national, organizational, or occupational. As you review the sections below, occupational cultures may pose the biggest challenges as we look ahead.

Realities About What Culture Is

Culture is the shared tacit assumptions of a group that have been learned through coping with external tasks and dealing with internal relationships.

Although culture manifests itself in artifacts such as overt behavior, rituals, climate, and espoused values, its essence is shared tacit assumptions that can be brought to consciousness—but that operate most of the time outside our awareness. As a responsible leader, you must be aware of those assumptions and manage them—or they will manage you.

The strength and depth of an *organization's* culture reflect (1) the strength and clarity of the founder of the organization; (2) the amount and intensity of shared experiences that organization members have had; and (3) the degree of success the organization has had.

Culture is, therefore, the *product* of social learning. Ways of thinking and behavior that are shared and *that work* become elements of the culture and, with continued success, become tacit assumptions about the way things are and ought to be.

The strength and depth of an *occupational* culture reflect the degree to which it is "professionalized" in the sense of requiring a prolonged period of education and/or apprenticeship to be licensed to perform as a member of that occupation and the length of time the occupation has successfully performed its function in the larger society. Thus members develop common assumptions from their educational and socialization experienced and come to think alike *even if they have not shared common experiences*.

Therefore, you cannot *"create"* a new culture in an organization that has already evolved a culture. You can demand or stimulate a new way of working together or a new way of thinking; you can monitor people to make sure that they are using the new ways, but members of the organization will not internalize new ways or working or thinking and make them part of the culture unless, over time, the new ways are actually better. The Amoco engineers did not give up the core of their engineering culture, even though the change program required them to behave differently and thus forced some new learning on top of their culture.

On the other hand, in these new forms of collaboration that are springing up, culture is being created because the organization is itself being created. Thus, task forces, joint ventures, and so on will create culture in terms of what leaders demand, what the group discovers from its own experience and, above all, what works in terms of getting the task done and managing internal relationships.

There is no absolute criterion for a "better" or a "worse" culture. A given organization's culture will be "right" for that organization as long as the organization succeeds in its primary task and can manage its internal relationships. If the organization begins to fail in accomplishing its primary task or if internal relationships break down, this means that some elements of the culture have become dysfunctional and will need to change or the organization may go out of existence. But the criterion of what is a *right* culture is always the pragmatic one of what enables the organization to succeed in its primary task and manage its internal relationships.

As the external and internal conditions of an organization change, so will the functionality or "rightness" of given cultural assumptions. Cultural elements then have to evolve with the evolving circumstances of the organization. Managing that cultural evolution is one of the primary tasks of leadership.

Realities About What Culture Covers

Once organizations have a culture, the shared tacit assumptions that make up that culture will influence *all* aspects of that organization's functioning. Mission, strategy, structure, means used, measurement systems, correction systems, language, group norms of inclusion and exclusion, status and reward systems, concepts of time, space, work, human nature, human relationships, and managing the unmanageable are all reflected in the culture.

It is especially important for you to understand that mission, strategy, and structure are all colored by cultural assumptions, even though most models of organizations show culture as an independent element. If you seek objectivity in those areas, you must find outsiders to work with you to help you identify your own cultural biases.

In the new organization each of the above content areas can be viewed as a culture creation problem and posed as a question. Can we get consensus on our mission, on how we will work together, how we will measure our progress, and how will we manage our internal power and intimacy relationships? The leader of the future must be aware that in a multicultural group the resolution of these issues can become a major stumbling block, especially around managing internal authority relationships.

Realities About Deciphering Culture

You cannot use a survey to assess culture. No survey will have enough questions to cover all of the relevant areas; individual employees will not know how to answer many of the questions and, even if they do provide data, you will not know what the salient elements of the culture are relative to some problem you might be trying to solve.

Culture is a group phenomenon. It is *shared* tacit assumptions. Therefore, the best way to assess cultural elements is to bring groups together to talk about their organization in a structured way that leads them to identify their own tacit assumptions. The best way to do this is to first identify all the artifacts pertaining to the area you are inquiring about, especially observed behavioral regularities. Compare these to the espoused values of the organization and, if they don't match, look for the tacit assumption that explains the behavior.

You can decipher your own cultural biases if you make yourself partially marginal in your own culture. "Travel" to other organizations (cultures) and work with consultants or colleagues from other organizations to reflect on your own tacit, taken-for-granted assumptions.

In the multicultural group the dilemma is how to assess multiple cultures simultaneously. The best bet is for the leader to get a sense of where there might be strong emotionally held differences and focus a dialogue on that area through a question that elicits behavioral data. For example, in one such group I asked the members to tell in order how each of their "home" organizations would handle it if their boss made a suggestion that they thought would lead to bad outcomes.

Realities About the Process of Culture Change

Any organizational culture change is transformative because you have to unlearn something before you can learn something new. The "unlearning" is painful and causes resistance to change.

The motivation to unlearn and learn something new comes from the realization that, if you continue in the present way, you will not achieve your goals; you will experience "survival anxiety." Survival anxiety is created by disconfirmation—information that something you want or expect is not happening or the wrong things are happening. That motivates you to do something else.

But the realization of what may be involved in learning something new causes "learning anxiety" because you realize that you may become temporarily incompetent, lose your current role, lose your membership in your group, or even lose your identity, if you learn something new. Resistance to change is a normal result of learning anxiety.

For change to occur, survival anxiety must be greater than learning anxiety, but just increasing survival anxiety does not work as long as learning anxiety is high because the disconfirming data can be denied, ignored, or rationalized away. Instead, the way to produce change is to lower learning anxiety through creating psychological safety for the learner.

Psychological safety is produced by providing a clear, non-negotiable credible vision of the future, clear targets of what the new behavior is to be, opportunities for the involvement of the learner in the process of learning, adequate training, resources in time and money for new learning, and structural supports in the way of congruent reward, control, and discipline systems.

If you are the agent of the change, the key to managing transformative change is to balance survival anxiety with enough psychological safety to overcome resistance.

Culture evolves and changes through several different mechanisms that you can influence to varying degrees:

- General evolution through adaptation to the environment
- Specific evolution of subgroups to their different environments
- Guided evolution resulting from cultural "insights" on the part of leaders
- Guided evolution through empowering selected hybrids from subcultures that are better adapted to current realities

- Planned and managed culture change through creation of parallel systems of steering committees and project-oriented task forces
- Partial or total cultural destruction through new leadership that eliminates the carriers of the former culture (turn-arounds, bankruptcies, etc.)

If you are in a young and growing organization, you can help to evolve and consolidate the culture, and you can help members gain insight into the culture. Remember that in a growing organization the culture is so central to the identity of the organization that changing elements of that culture becomes very difficult. If you have time, you can evolve the culture by looking for leaders who have arisen in the various subcultures, locating those who hold the kinds of assumptions you feel are needed and promoting them into more powerful positions.

If you are in a mid-life organization that has clearly dysfunctional elements in its culture, you may launch a managed change program by creating a parallel system to assess the culture, identify a change program, and implement it. Planned change programs hinge on a clear and non-negotiable vision of what the new kind of behavior is to be and the involvement of the employees in figuring out how to get there. Employee involvement is the best way of ensuring a degree of psychological safety. If the new behavior produces better results, it will eventually lead to internalization of the values it is based on and will eventually become an element of the culture.

If you are in a mid-life or aging organization that has dysfunctional elements in the core culture and you do not have time for a managed change program, you may need to function as a turnaround manager, assess the culture to identify the dysfunctional elements, locate the carriers of those cultural elements you do not want, and replace them. This will be a painful process. Alternatively you may need to destroy the organization through bankruptcy, a merger, or an acquisition that forces major reassessment of cultural elements.

Realities About the Timing of Culture Assessment and Change

Never start with the idea of changing a culture. Always start with the issues the organization faces, and only when those "business" issues are clear, ask yourself whether the culture will aid or hinder resolving the issues. Now is the time to do a culture assessment.

Always think first of the culture as your source of strength. It is the residue of your past successes. Even if some elements of the culture now look dysfunctional, remember that those are likely to be only a few elements in a very large set of elements that continue to be strengths.

If major changes need to be made in the way the organization is run, try to build on the existing cultural strengths, rather than trying to change those elements that may be weaknesses.

Realities About Mergers, Acquisitions, Joint Ventures, and Collaborations

Where members of different cultures have come together to create something new, an entirely different approach must be used. For one thing, it is rarely possible to study the "other cultures" well enough to predict how working together will actually play out. Therefore it is necessary to create shared events in which people can become acquainted before any work output is required.

The reality is that everyone believes in his or her own culture and way of doing things. The goal in any multicultural collaboration must therefore be the creation of a new culture built out of joint learning by the new group members. Even in mergers and acquisitions where domination, separation, blending or conflict are possible initial responses, the new organization will not function effectively until it has evolved cultural elements that are based on new learning experiences from group members working together.

If you are the leader of a multicultural collaboration, first train yourself in being culturally sensitive by visiting other organizations or cultures and trying to figure out how their assumptions differ from yours. Develop your "cultural intelligence." When the members of the group are first together, create activities that allow informal acquaintance and back these up with Dialogue sessions during which members can reflect on their new joint experiences or review their own prior cultural experiences around focused questions such as the one suggested above about authority relationships.

Do not expect that good will and joint experience will be enough to produce mutual *understanding*. Each member needs to learn to be reflective—to get in touch with his or her own assumptions—and this can only be done with the Dialogue format. Because we don't know where globalism and technological evolution (especially in information technology) will lead us, the culture leader of the future must be prepared to be more culturally intelligent—more motivated to understand others and more flexible in his or her own behavioral repertoire.

A Final Thought

Learning about culture requires effort. You have to enlarge your perception, you have to examine your own thought process, you have to accept that there are other ways to think and do things. But once you have acquired what I would call a "cultural perspective,," what is increasingly being labeled as "cultural intelligence" you will be amazed at how rewarding it is. Suddenly, the world is much clearer. Anomalies are now explainable, conflicts are more understandable, resistance to change begins to look normal, and, most important, your own humility increases. And in that humility you will find wisdom and an increased capacity to work with others whose thoughts and feelings may be very different from yours.

Notes

Chapter One

1. A detailed analysis of the rise and fall of DEC is in Schein, E. H., et al., 2003.
2. This story is based on extensive interviews with Richard Beckhard, who was one of the main consultants to the project, and members of the P & G project team.
3. Roth, G., 1993.
4. Snook, S. A., 2000.
5. Gerstein, M., 2008; Vaughan, D., 1996.
6. Martin, J., & Siehl, C., 1983.
7. Salk, J., 1997.

Chapter Three

1. Cameron, K. S., & Quinn, R. E., 1999; Goffee, R., & Jones, G., 1998.
2. In a longitudinal study of careers, it was found that people develop a self-concept of what drives their career and constrains career choices (Schein, 2006). Eight anchors were identified: Autonomy, Security, Technical/Functional Competence, General Managerial Competence, Entrepreneurial Creativity, Service, Pure Challenge, and Life Style.

Chapter Four

1. Most useful for this purpose are the dimensions used originally by Kluckhohn & Strodtbeck (1961). Several of these dimensions have also been found in big international studies comparing country variations in a single organization such as IBM (Hofstede, 2001).
2. McGregor, D., 1960.
3. Hall, E. T., 1959; 1966.
4. Extensive research on the concept of polychronicity and how it relates to other dimensions of culture has been done by Bluedorn (2000).
5. Dubinskas (1988) has shown how this variable is crucial in the evolution of young biotech firms.
6. Jaques, E., 1982.
7. Barley, S. R., 1988.

Chapter Five

1. Cameron, K. S., & Quinn, R. E., 1999.
2. Goffee, R., & Jones, G., 1988.
3. Sackman, S. A., & Bertelsmann Stiftung, 2006.
4. Schein, E. H., 1996; Van Maanen, J., & Barley, S. R., 1984.

Chapter Six

1. This model was originally formulated by Kurt Lewin in the 1940s and has since been elaborated and used widely in managing change projects (Lewin, 1947; Schein, 1961).
2. Coghlan, D., & Rashford, N. S., 2006.

Chapter Seven

1. Gerstner, L. V., 2002.
2. Dyer, W. G., 1986.
3. Schein, E. H., 1996.
4. Thomas, R. J., 1994.
5. Tedlow, R. S., 2003.

Chapter Eight

1. Bushe, G. R., & Shani, A. B., 1991; Zand, D. E., 1974.

Chapter Nine

1. Roth, G., & Kleiner, A., 2000.
2. Kotter, J. P., & Heskett, J. L., 1992; Tichy, N. M., & Devanna, M. A., 1986.
3. Schein, E. H., 2003.
4. Gerstner, L. V., 2002; Young, J. S., & Simon, W. L., 2005.
5. Schein, E. H., 1987, 1999.

Chapter Ten

1. A recent example is described in great detail in Fadiman's 1997 account of how U.S. doctors and Hmong patients had communication difficulties.
2. Buono, A. F., & Bowditch, J. L., 1989; McManus, M. L., & Hergert, M. L., 1988; *Harvard Business Review on Mergers and Acquisitions*, 2001.
3. Gibson, C. B., & Dibble, R., 2008, pp. 222–223.
4. Busco, C., Riccaboni, A., & Scapens, R. W., 2002.
5. Salk, J., 1997.
6. Gerstein, M., 2008.
7. Ang, S., & Van Dyne, L., 2008.
8. Dougherty, D., 2001.
9. Hofstede, G., 2001.
10. Edmondson, A. C., Bohmer, R. M., & Pisano, G. P., 2001.
11. Dougherty, D., 2001.
12. Isaacs, W., 1993, 1999; Schein, E. H., 1993.

Chapter Eleven

1. Mirvis, P., Ayas, K., & Roth, G., 2003.

References

Ang, S., & Van Dyne, L. (Eds.). (2008). *Handbook of cultural intelligence.* Armonk, NY: M.E. Sharpe.

Barley, S. R. (1988). "On technology, time, and social order." In F. A. Dubinskas (Ed.), *Making time.* Philadelphia: Temple University Press.

Beckhard, R., & Harris, R. T. (1987). *Organizational transitions* (2nd ed.) Reading, MA: Addison-Wesley.

Bluedorn, A. C. (2000). "Time and organizational culture." In N. M. Ashkanazy, C. P. M. Wilderom, & M. F. Peterson (Eds.), *Handbook of organizational culture and climate.* Thousand Oaks, CA: Sage.

Buono, A. F., & Bowditch, J. L. (1989). *The human side of mergers and acquisitions.* San Francisco: Jossey-Bass.

Bushe, G. R., & Shani, A. B. (1991). *Parallel learning structures.* Englewood Cliffs, NJ: Prentice-Hall.

Busco, C., Riccaboni, A., & Scapens, R. W. (2002). When culture matters: Management accounting change within process of organizational learning and transformation. *Reflections, 4*(1), 43–54.

Cameron, K. S., & Quinn, R. E. (1999). *Diagnosing and changing organizational culture.* Englewood Cliffs, NJ: Prentice-Hall.

Coghlan, D., & Rashford, N. S. (2006). *Organizational change and strategy.* London: Routledge.

Dubinskas, F. A. (Ed.). (1988). *Making time.* Philadelphia: Temple University Press.

Dougherty, D. (2001). Re-imagining the differentiation and integration of work for sustained product innovation. *Organization Science, 12*(5), 612–631.

Dyer, W. G. Jr. (1986). *Culture change in family firms.* San Francisco: Jossey-Bass.

Edmondson, A. C., Bohmer, R. M., & Pisano, G. P. (2001). Disrupted routines: Team learning and new technology implementation in hospitals. *Administrative Science Quarterly, 46,* 685–716.

Fadiman, A. (1997). *The spirit catches you and you fall down.* New York: Farrar, Straus & Giroux.

Gerstein, M. (2008). *Flirting with disaster.* New York: Union Square.

Gerstner, L. V. (2002). *Who says elephants can't dance?* New York: HarperCollins.

Gibson, C. B., & Dibble, R. (2008). "Culture inside and out: Developing a collaboration's capacity to externally adapt." In S. Ang & L. Van Dyne (Eds.), *Handbook of cultural intelligence.* Armonk, NY: M. E. Sharpe, pp. 222–223.

Goffee, R., & Jones, G. (1998). *The character of a corporation.* New York: Harper Business.

Hall, E. T. (1959). *The silent language.* New York: Doubleday.

Hall, E. T. (1966). *The hidden dimension.* New York: Doubleday.

Harvard Business Review on mergers and acquisitions. (2001). Boston, MA: Harvard Business Press.

Hofstede, G. (2001). *Culture's consequences* (2nd ed.). Thousand Oaks, CA: Sage.

Isaacs, W. (1999). *Dialogue and the art of thinking together.* New York: Doubleday.

Jaques, E. (1982). *The forms of time.* London: Heinemann.

Kluckhohn, F. R., & Strodtbeck, F. L. (1961). *Variations in value orientations.* New York: HarperCollins.

Kotter, J. P., & Heskett, J. L. (1992). *Culture and performance.* New York: Free Press.

Lewin, K. (1947). "Group decision and social change." In T. N. Newcomb & E. L. Hartley (Eds.), *Readings in social psychology.* New York: Holt, Rinehart and Winston.

Martin, J., & Siehl, C. (1983). Organizational culture and counterculture: An uneasy symbiosis. *Organizational Dynamics, 12,* 52–64.

McGregor, D. (1960). *The human side of enterprise.* New York: McGraw-Hill.

McManus, M. L., & Hergert, M. L. (1988). *Surviving merger and acquisition.* Glencoe, IL: Scott Foresman.

Mirvis, P., Ayas, K., & Roth, G. (2003). *To the desert and back.* San Francisco: Jossey-Bass.

Roth, G. (1993). In search of the paperless office. Unpublished Ph.D. dissertation. Cambridge, MA: MIT Sloan School of Management.

Roth, G., & Kleiner, A. (2000). *Car launch: The human side of managing change.* New York: Oxford University Press.

Sackman, S. A., & Bertelsmann Stiftung (2006). *Success factor: Corporate culture.* Bielefeld, Germany: Bertlemann Stiftung.

Salk, J. (1997). Partners and other strangers. *International Studies of Management and Organization, 26*(4), 48–72.

Schein, E. H. (1961). *Coercive persuasion.* New York: Norton.

Schein, E. H. (1987). *Process consultation* (Vol. 1) Englewood Cliffs, NJ: Prentice-Hall.

Schein, E. H. (1993, Autumn). On dialogue, culture, and organizational learning. *Organizational Dynamics, 22,* 40–51.

Schein, E. H. (1996). Three cultures of management. *Sloan Management Review, 38*(1), 9–20.

Schein, E. H. (1999). *Process consultation revisited.* Englewood Cliffs, NJ: Prentice Hall.

Schein, E. H. with P. S. DeLisi, P. J. Kampas, & M. M. Sonduck. (2003). *DEC is dead; Long live DEC: The lasting legacy of Digital Equipment Corporation.* San Francisco: Berrett-Koehler.

Schein, E. H. (2006). *Career anchors* (3rd ed.). San Francisco: Pfeiffer.

Snook, S. A. (2000). *Friendly fire.* Princeton, NJ: Princeton University Press.

Tedlow, R. S. (2003). *The Watson dynasty* New York: Harper Business.

Thomas, R. J. (1994). *What machines can't do.* Berkeley, CA: University of California Press.

Tichy, N. M., & Devanna, M. A. (1986). *The transformational leader.* Hoboken, NJ: John Wiley & Sons.

Vaughan, D. (1996). *The Challenger launch decision.* Chicago: University of Chicago Press.

Van Maanen, J., & Barley, S. R. (1984). "Occupational communities: Culture and control in organizations. In B. M. Staw & L. L. Cummings (Eds.), *Research in organizational behavior* (Vol. 6). Greenwich, CT: JAI Press.

Young, J. S., & Simon, W. L. (2005). *iCon Steve Jobs.* Hoboken, NJ: John Wiley & Sons.

Zand, D. E. (1974). Collateral organization: A new change strategy. *Journal of Applied Behavioral Science, 10,* 63–89.

Index

Page references followed by *e* indicate an exhibit; followed by *fig* indicate an illustrated figure.